MULBERRY
The material culture of mulberry trees

S.J. Bowe

MORVS

TARDE MORIES

MORVM

CITO

MORITVR

To my father Joseph and
my mother Mary

First published 2015 by
Liverpool University Press
4 Cambridge Street
Liverpool
L69 7ZU

British Library Cataloguing-in-Publication data
A British Library CIP record is available

ISBN 978-1-78138-243-1

Designed by Carnegie Book Production
Printed and bound by Gutenberg Press Ltd, Malta

Cover image: *Mulberries, Wine and Cheese* (2014) by
Trisha Hardwick (reversed). Courtesy of the artist.

LIVERPOOL
UNIVERSITY PRESS

Contents

List of Illustrations

Foreword

Peter Goodwin

Furniture and treen makers in Britain have always known that the wood from *Morus nigra*, the black mulberry tree, held very desirable qualities, such as the complex grain patterns, high chance of burr configuration and a golden colour which gradually darkens with time. Trying to acquire such rare wood was quite another matter because the trees are usually growing in important places and treasured by their owners. Even in old age the mulberry tree is always the first to receive attention – being propped up and cosseted for years (when other tree species would be removed). So it was not until the 'hurricane' of 1987 that mulberry wood was suddenly on the lumber market. Specialist furniture makers like John Makepeace, David Linley, myself and others soon realised there was an opportunity to collect and store mulberry wood.

In my case, offers of windblown mulberries came from a variety of sources: the Georgian manor with the tree in front of the house, the country cottage with a tree in the vegetable garden, a mulberry in a walled back garden, trees in city squares and a military college which had a row of ten fallen mulberry trees. Many of the owners had significant stories to tell and wanted their trees to be used to create something memorable – such as furniture. Titchmarsh & Goodwin gave the owners a small treen item turned by Richard Chapman as a complimentary memento. To this day, John Makepeace seeks out any piece of mulberry wood that he can find and has created a number of mulberry pieces that often appear in *Woodland Heritage* (Illustration 1).

This story, and the creation of other mulberry wood items, are featured in this publication and, in addition, the work also acknowledges the supreme talents of Japanese craft makers who have been supported and befriended by the author. He has amassed a unique knowledge of the mulberry trees that grow on the remote Japanese Izu islands, and this wonderful book gives the reader an insight into the traditions and styles of their furniture and smaller wooden items. Stephen has produced research of real quality that will be the cornerstone of future work on mulberry trees and their material culture.

Preface

Mulberry: the Material Culture of Mulberry Trees is a study in five chapters focusing on the material culture of mulberry trees. The approach was adopted from one that the Winterthur Museum in the USA used to interpret the artefacts featured in various informational exhibitions. The first chapter looks at the location of mulberry trees in England and Wales along with some contextual information. The second chapter analyses mulberry-related material produced in the decorative and fine arts. The pivotal third chapter focuses on mulberry furniture produced by two companies – Titchmarsh & Goodwin in the United Kingdom and Kichizo in Japan. The fourth chapter highlights numerous rituals and customs while discussing the various craft traditions that underpin the making of mulberry-related items, such as those used in the tea ceremony. Finally, literary and scientific associations are featured with specific reference to those mulberry wood items that are connected with William Shakespeare.

Acknowledgements

This book is dedicated to my parents. It is interesting that concurrent research on the Bowe family tree has reached back to ancestors who lived in the reign of James VI and I; both mulberry trees and my family of Wensleydale Quakers have a recorded history in a similar time frame.

Mulberry: the Material Culture of Mulberry Trees has taken a long time to come to fruition and there are hundreds of people and institutions that require a thank you. Here are a few, in no particular order.

People: Roger Saul, John Makepeace, Andrew Kirk, Alison Welsby, Martin Gee, Reg Phillips, Emma Roberts, Ian Wroot, Trisha Hardwick, Mary Restieaux, Anthony Malone, Peter Goodwin and Yoshitaka Sugiyama. Companies: Mulberry, Morris & Co., Zoffany, Hermès, Sanderson, Vitra, Tiptree Preserves, Tichelaar Makkum, John Mitchell & Sons and Whittington Press.

In addition, thanks to all the guardians of the gardens that feature in the study who willingly provided a substantial amount of contextual material, and to the museums and galleries that provided information that helped with the research.

Finally, thanks to Liverpool John Moores University, which provided the funds in order to complete the project and exhibit the material.

Change over Space

Introduction

The mulberry is part of the kingdom *Plantae*, and belongs to the phylum *Magnoliophyta*, class *Magnoliopsida*, order *Rosales*, family *Moraceae* and the genus *Morus*. Species include *Morus nigra* (black mulberry), *Morus alba* (white mulberry) and *Morus rubra* (red mulberry). Mulberry trees grow throughout the world (see Illustration 2) and there are specific words for mulberry in different languages – French (*mure*), German (*maulbeere*), Spanish (*mura*), Italian (*mura*), Portuguese (*amoreira*), Danish (*morbaer*), Norwegian (*morbaer*), Swedish (*mullbar*), Finnish (*mulperi*), Russian (*shelkovitsa/tutovaya yagoda*), Polish (*morwa*), Serbo-Croat (*dud/murva*), Romanian (*duda*), Bulgarian (*cherhitsa*), Greek (*moran/mouro*), Turkish (*dut*), Hebrew/Persian (*tut*), Arabic (*tut aswad*), Indonesian (*bebesaran*), Chinese (*sang shen*) and finally Japanese (*kuwa*). This study is concerned with the mulberry tree, and considers its significance in the United Kingdom before making a comparative study of its importance in Japan.

There has been a well-documented association between human beings and trees throughout history.[1] Trees have a significant bearing on our well-being, giving us wood for shelter, food, useful substances (including paper, rubber and aspirin) plus oxygen via photosynthesis. The importance of trees to our contemporary daily lives has been brought into focus by global warming and climate change.

Trees not only offer us numerous benefits but also provide complete ecosystems throughout the world and are clearly critical for life on the planet. Some trees are natural or native and flourish without the intervention of man, while others are nurtured and planted for their aesthetic and functional purposes. In the United Kingdom, certain trees are planted for harvest, including orchard trees such as the medlar, plum, greengage, apple, pear, quince, cherry, damson, walnut, cobnut and mulberry. In fact some of the mulberry trees in this study can be found in orchards and are located by other fruit trees; for example, the tree at Carlton Hall is near both damson and medlar trees (Survey List 73), while a tree at Erddig Hall is associated with multiple varieties of fruit including fig and medlar (Survey List 6). Erddig is famous for its heritage fruit collection including espalier pears and cordoned apples, which grow amongst pleached limes (*Tilia x euchlora*).

The impact of trees on our daily lives was in part explored in an exhibition at the Whitworth Art Gallery, Manchester in 2010 entitled *Deep Rooted: How Trees Shape Our Lives*.[2] In many ways the mulberry is the perfect example of a productive tree in the fact that first it is used for food – the fruit being harvested for human consumption. The tree's leaves can be utilised both for animal feed and importantly to nurture silkworms (*Bombyx mori*) for the production

of silk.[3] The wood of the mulberry – like other fruitwoods – is used for both furniture and treen.[4] In short, the mulberry tree has a material culture that provides an interesting, indeed fascinating, subject for discussion.

Mulberry trees are highly regarded by their owners (as evidenced by numerous letters and detailed correspondence received during research for this study) and the histories attached to the trees can in some cases be documented over hundreds of years. In the United Kingdom, mulberry trees are nearly always found in domestic settings and are often associated with historic houses. In many cases they have achieved listed status and are protected in law. Many local authorities and councils have specialist staff (sometimes arboriculturists) who monitor mulberry trees with tree preservation orders – for example, West Lancashire District Council has an order on a mulberry tree at Normanhurst in Ormskirk, Lancashire. This tree, identified as T17 in Order Number 32 (2003), is a survivor of a modern development of eight houses and is a relic of the Victorian house which originally stood on the site.[5] There are examples in the Survey List of trees that have been left stranded by modern developments, which is the case with the mulberry at Croxteth Hall on Merseyside (Survey List 71), which is now very difficult to find. It is on the perimeter of a fenced car park near the hall and is hidden amongst other trees and shrubs. Some Environmental Services departments also have a number of mulberry trees with protection orders – for example, the Royal Borough of Kingston upon Thames has a total of 17 protected mulberry trees,[6] far more than you would expect for just one species. A subsidiary survey (not reported in depth) of preservation orders throughout the United Kingdom revealed that many councils have mulberry trees that require conservation and protection – often relics or sole survivors of past houses or established gardens (for example, the John Evelyn mulberry tree at Sayes Court featured below in Chapter 5).

Some mulberry trees can appear in relative isolation, such as the Groton Winthrop tree, which is located in a meadow and is significant enough to be cared for by a trust. This black mulberry tree was planted in the lifetime of Adam Winthrop (1498–1562), probably around 1550. He was the grandfather of puritan John Winthrop (1588–1649) who established the first permanent settlement in the USA and later became the inaugural Governor of Massachusetts. In 1993, the field in which the tree was established was overgrown and the

parish council raised funds to purchase the plot of land from the Revd Tony Moore for £8,500 in order to fence off the tree and protect it. As a result, a trust fund was set up in New York so that descendants of the Winthrop family could protect their heritage. In fact one member of the Winthrop family, also named John, made a pilgrimage to see the tree in 1978 and on his return to Boston planted a black mulberry tree on Boston Common in 1980. The tradition of planting *Morus nigra* continues in the USA.[7]

The material culture of the mulberry has been documented in literature and more recently on television. The television series *Meetings with Remarkable Trees* looked at numerous famous trees in the United Kingdom, including a mulberry tree ostensibly planted by John Milton (1608–1674) in the grounds of a Cambridge college (Survey List 7).[8] The tree is now over 400 years old. It is nurtured for aesthetic reasons but also because the fruit is harvested for the college, and the tree has become a tourist attraction in its own right. It has reached a significance beyond its material existence and has become a treasured member of the college and its environs. Its history has many twists and turns but it is thought that the tree was originally associated with an edict by James I (the first of the Stuart monarchs) in around 1609 that encouraged the planting of mulberry trees in the United Kingdom so that silk could be produced for the royal court. A portrait by Johan de Critz (1605) shows James in his finery, wearing what appears to be silk, and this can be viewed at the Dulwich Picture Gallery.

There is a street called Mulberry Walk off the Kings Road in London that delineated the southern boundary of Chelsea Park and which was the area, along with St James's Park and Buckingham Palace gardens, in which James I planted his mulberry trees for silk cultivation. It is assumed that James supervised the planting of a significant number of trees in the grounds of his hunting park. Bonham Bazeley in *The Garden* writes:

> In an effort to enliven the economy James set an example by planting 1.62 hectares (4 acres) of mulberries, which the diarists John Evelyn and Samuel Pepys both mentioned, on land now occupied by Buckingham Palace and its garden. James also ordered 100,000 mulberry trees from France and in November, 1609, he required a number of his Lords-Lieutenant to organise the

2 Swedish mulberry tree illustration (1978), by Eva Stockhaus

planting of 10,000 trees in their counties, to be collected from the City of London, for which they had to pay the subsidised price of three farthings each.[9]

James also persuaded his courtiers to plant mulberry trees, including those at Theobalds in Cheshunt, Hatfield in Hertfordshire, Weathersdane Hall in Kent, Broadlands in Hampshire and Charlton House in London. Of the tree at Charlton House, Jo Stokes and Donald Rodger write in *Heritage Trees of Britain and Northern Ireland*:

> It is probably the first planted after the 'Order' from King James since it stands in the grounds of Charlton House, in Greenwich, London. The house was built by Adam Newton, tutor to King James's eldest son Prince Henry. It is probable that Newton planted the tree at the start of the King's mulberry promotion. This mulberry is certainly one of the oldest known to be still growing.[10]

Charlton House is a Jacobean mansion attributed to John Thorpe (1560–1620), one of the earliest known British architects, and was built between 1607 and 1612 for Sir Adam Newton. The house featured in *Country Life* in 1909 when the Maryon-Wilson family was still in residence.[11] After a chequered history, the house and grounds were purchased by the Metropolitan Borough of Greenwich in 1925. Sadly, the mulberry has a rather miserable and isolated position, but remains alive and in relatively good condition in a fenced compound. However, the king's project appears not to have been completely successful, as silkworms, while being able to eat black mulberry leaves, show a preference for the softer white mulberry. Nevertheless, rather than being a mistake (as many report), it may be that planting the black mulberry was decided upon because white mulberries are more prone to United Kingdom winters and can prove delicate. In terms of silk production the experiment appears to have been a failure, although apparently Anne of Denmark (1574–1619) did have a dress woven from indigenous UK silk.

A piece of woven silk fabric (from Italy) with silver metal thread is featured in the collections of the Victoria & Albert Museum (V&A) (Museum Number T.361-1970). This fabric features peacock feathers, not unlike the iconic Hera fabric produced for Liberty & Co. Anne of Denmark, queen consort of James I, wore a similar fabric, as shown in a portrait by Marcus Gheeraerts the Younger (1561/62–1636) – peacock feathers being appropriate for a queen because they are associated with Juno, the wife of Jupiter, king of the Roman gods. English-reared silk has become a tradition for celebration garments for the Royal Family. For example, Princess Diana had silk of UK origin in her wedding dress in 1981, provided by Compton House. Lady Hart Dyke started a silk farm in the 1930s at Lullingstone Castle where silkworms were reared on Osigian mulberry from Venezuela, which has enormous leaves that are both soft and palatable for the insects. It takes many tonnes of mulberry leaves to make a relatively small amount of the final product. The silkworms will digest black mulberry leaves but it is now well established that white mulberry species produce a better-quality silk. Lullingstone silk was used for the coronation robes for Elizabeth II in 1953. The farm closed in 1977 after the death of Lady Hart Dyke in 1975.[12] *Bombyx mori* is not the only insect from which silk is harvested – the V&A in 2012 exhibited a magnificent and unique golden cape made from the silk of over 1 million female golden orb weaver spiders (*Nephila madagascarensis*) from Madagascar. The cape was made in 2011 by Simon Peers and Nicholas Godley and will be discussed in greater detail in Chapter 2.

There is a collection of mulberry trees of varying ages housed at Buckingham Palace and Kensington Palace that comprises some 29 species. These are mostly young trees and mainly *Morus alba*. The Royal Family in 1996 became the guardians of the national collection of mulberry trees under the auspices of the National Council for the Conservation of Plants and Gardens (NCCPG), which includes a 110-year-old black mulberry over 13 metres high. Other, younger examples of *Morus* species include a *Morus bombycis* Koidzumi planted in 1993. According to the gardener at Buckingham Palace, the fruits are not used by the palace but are instead gathered by the blackbirds.[13] Blackbirds are known to adore the fruits and find them irresistible – interestingly, this features in a plasterwork decoration at Plas Mawr, in North Wales.

Mulberry trees are relatively common in the United Kingdom and can be purchased in garden centres, and they have been recommended by contemporary gardeners such as Dan Pearson.[14] Garden centres have produced mulberry cultivars, such as Illinois Everbearing, which is a vigorous plant with good fruit and disease

resistance. Traditional varieties such as Chelsea (named after the mulberry in the Chelsea Physic Garden), Charlton (after the black mulberry at the house) and King James (after James I) can still be purchased as small trees. Furthermore, on his website, the television chef and writer Rick Stein has recommended mulberry jam from Wilkin & Sons of Tiptree, Essex and produced a recipe using fresh mulberries for poached pears and mulberries with mascarpone ice cream.[15] Food writer Nigel Slater has grown a black mulberry in his garden which fruited for the first time in 2009 (after nine years).[16] Nigella Lawson has a community recipe for mulberry sauce on her website[17] and mulberry juice has been mentioned in the television programme *The Great British Bake Off*.[18]

The mulberry tree is part of the family *Moraceae* and is related to other productive species such as the fig (*Ficus carica*), breadfruit (*Artocarpus altilis*) and the osage orange tree (*Maclura pomifera*). The paper mulberry (*Broussonetia papyrifera*) is grown in Japan for its fibre, which is used to make high-quality paper such as washi. As with all trees, the mulberry is not solely one variety but a collection of species with a very complex nomenclature. However, the simple division, which is very easy to remember, is that there are three main species – the black mulberry (sometimes called the Persian mulberry), the white mulberry (sometimes called the Russian mulberry) and the red mulberry (sometimes called the American mulberry).

This study is mainly concerned with the black mulberry in the United Kingdom and the white mulberry in Japan. The black mulberry is nearly always associated with horticulture in the United Kingdom while those in Japan are often associated with agriculture and can even be found in the wild. The book *Fruit*, produced in association with the Royal Horticultural Society, is an illustrated history of many fruit species, including tropical and unusual fruits.[19] It details varieties, propagation and some historical context relating to both common and very rare varieties. The book includes the black mulberry, *Morus nigra*, and contains an illustration of the variety *Murier de Virginie*. It also features the white mulberry, *Morus alba*, and the red mulberry, *Morus rubra*, which is found largely in the USA. The book states that the mulberry has pips instead of a stone and is part of the family *Moraceae*, which is a plant family with about 1,850 species found throughout the world. In terms of genetics, the black mulberry has few species but rather simple clones. The origin of the black mulberry is given as Central Asia. It is mentioned in the Bible and it has been cultivated in the Mediterranean for thousands of years. Pliny remarks on the staining of the fruit, and it is likely that the mulberry tree was introduced into the United Kingdom during the Roman occupation. A more comprehensive history is given in John Feltwell's *The Story of Silk*.[20]

In *Fruit*, we further read:

> A mulberry tree's most important virtue is the ripe old age to which it will grow. There are accounts of several that have exceeded six hundred years – one of which was planted at the Drapers' Hall in the City of London in 1364 and only died in 1969. Another early tree is thought to have been planted at Silent House – the seat of the Duke of Northumberland in 1548.[21]

Drapers' Hall was established over 600 years ago and is now associated with various charities including almshouses. The first charter for the Drapers was granted in 1364 but it was formally established in 1516. The fraternity started even earlier, as a religious group known as the Brotherhood of Drapers, and has since developed into one of the wealthiest and most influential of the livery companies in the City of London alongside the Mercers and Grocers.[22] The first Drapers' Hall was located in St Swithin's Lane but moved in 1543 to a site in Throgmorton Street, which also had an associated garden. The original building was destroyed during the Great Fire of London in 1666 and rebuilt between 1667 and 1671 and this building was progressively rebuilt and altered into the Victorian period. The garden is relatively small and was reorganised in the 1970s on a very well-established plot of land. The garden contains both old and younger mulberry trees, some of which were planted by Queen Elizabeth II and Prince Charles. The trees are nurtured and cared for and were the subject of a report by a tree surgeon in 2000, which mentioned five trees. Tree one was a mature *Morus nigra* tree with a height of 9 metres and a trunk diameter of 36 cm. The crown covered approximately 3 metres but some of the branches were dead and re-pollarding was recommended. Tree two was also a black mulberry, 8 metres high, with a trunk diameter of 23 cm. Like tree one, this tree was in poor condition, and the tree surgeon recommended severe pruning and the possible planting of a replacement. Tree three was an uncommon mulberry that has been identified as *Morus kagayamae*, which is usually a native of Japan, and this will be discussed further in later chapters. A fourth tree was described as a middle-aged tree with similar dimensions to trees one and two, but it had greater vigour, spanning some 10 metres at its crown. There was also a smaller tree, which

was described as a sapling.[23] All the trees are in a designated conservation area and are located in a relatively built-up area that is very near to the Bank of England in Threadneedle Street. The Bank also has associated mulberry trees in its courtyard that were apparently planted by Sir Herbert Baker in the 1940s. They are thought to have been grown to signify the use of mulberry-bark paper in currency – the Chinese produced denominated money in the fourteenth century on the beaten bark of mulberry trees.[24] In *The Story of Silk* it is suggested that these trees may have been the descendants of a tree planted by the Huguenot Sir John Houblon (1632–1712), who founded the Bank of England in 1694.[25]

The taxonomy of the mulberry is complex, and *Morus* species are deciduous trees which are thought to have originated in the Himalayas. In the main it is associated economically with silk production and the various species used are genotypically variable, as inter-specific hybridisation often results in fertile strains. Modern genetic research has been useful in defining species but in the main the taxonomy has yet to be fully resolved.[26] The tree is now common in various climatic zones and is essentially found throughout the world. The trees grow reasonably well in temperate climatic conditions including the United Kingdom and Japan.[27] However, in the United Kingdom, *Morus nigra* is most common in the southern counties, becoming rarer further north and is fairly scarce in Scotland. Complex scientific research using cluster analysis and dendrograms has provided interesting material that identified certain species with a common ancestry being classified into Indian and Japanese types.[28] The Japanese white mulberry is dealt with in greater depth below in Chapters 3 and 4.

The black mulberry has a number of interesting characteristics, which include its ability to root and survive. It is recorded that a tree at Bruce Castle at Tottenham was grown from a large branch which had been torn off a tree by high winds and was simply buried in the ground to form a new and thriving tree. It is common for mulberry trees to 'wander' and they can often be found many metres away from their original planting site, as evidenced by John Feltwell: 'There is a fine example of this in the East Sussex parish of Rodmell, near Lewes, where there is a grove of what appears to be about thirty mulberry trees. In fact it is one tree that has collapsed, grown further on its "knuckles", collapsed again and grown yet more trees.'[29] This phenomenon is evidenced in this study at various properties, including Charlecote Park

(Survey List 13), Melford Hall (Survey List 25), Broadlands (Survey List 35) and Swallowfield Park (Survey List 57). It is common for black mulberry trees to fall over and re-root, and they often grow at an angle away from the vertical (see Survey List 3, 11, 17, 36 and 61). A tree not featured in the survey but with a very marked lean is the black mulberry found at Lesnes Abbey, which is virtually horizontal.

It is generally thought that the black mulberry will not produce fruit until it is at least fifteen years old, but this is not always the case, with young trees (three years old) producing fruit in certain circumstances. It is also said that the leaves of the black mulberry are the last to appear in late spring and the first to fade in autumn. When the leaves do form or open the process is said to be so vigorous that the move from bud to leaf can be heard at night. The leaves of the mulberry tree vary within species, those from the white mulberry being generally softer and often heart shaped. Sometimes biomorphic leaf shapes exist and the mulberry can produce leaf forms similar to the fig (*Ficus carica*). In addition, the leaves of the black mulberry can be very large (bigger than a hand span) and tend not to be predated by insects or subject to other plant diseases – probably because of the white latex-like substance found within the sap. A succinct account of the various mulberry trees can be found in *The Story of Silk*.[30] The fruit is botanically not a berry but a collective fruit, or drupe, which in *Morus nigra* has the appearance of a swollen loganberry or large blackberry (Illustration 3). The fruit of *Morus alba* and *Morus rubra* is not as large, and in the case of the white mulberry is often small and indistinct. The fruit of *Morus nigra* seems to ripen over a period of time rather than all at once and the black mulberry is often characterised by a 'sea' of dark stains on the ground under the crown of the tree. The stain from the fruit is notorious for the depth and extent of the colour. This staining in certain cases has resulted in the removal of trees such as was the case with Lambeth Council, which removed two young but fruiting trees (against much protest) that had been planted in what was part of the Vauxhall Pleasure Gardens in London.[31]

The mulberry tree is self-fertile and crops each year, and the trees will thrive in most soils. They are quite large, growing up to 9 metres in height and often being wider than they are tall, suggesting that they are not best suited for small gardens. The fruit does not survive well and its delicate nature means it is not found in commercial markets – this means that it is best grown at home.[32] Possibly the best way to sample the flavour of the fruit is in the juice produced by Fairjuice called Mulberry Fair – the company claims that it contains an antioxidant Resveratrol, having higher levels than blueberry or cranberry. Some restaurants, hotels and inns have attached mulberry trees, including the Manor House Hotel at Moreton-in-Marsh in the Cotswolds, which has a tree thought to be 300 years old that they harvest, utilising the fruit in their Mulberry Restaurant to make a cake, jam (for afternoon tea) and a syrup to use in cocktails. The George at Stamford in Lincolnshire – a famous historic coaching inn – has a considerable black mulberry tree in its grounds which features in its literature (Survey List 19). The history of the coaching inn is significant; a plaque on the wall states:

> In medieval times the house of
> the Holy Sepulchre stood on this
> site [&] knights of Saint John
> of Jerusalem were entertained
> here. In the garden at the rear
> crusaders in their black robes
> with white cross walked and
> talked. The gnarled mulberry tree
> dates from the time of James I.
> The main block of the hotel was
> erected in 1597 by Lord Burghley
> Lord High Treasurer to Queen
> Elizabeth I. At least three kings
> and many famous travellers have
> stayed here.

The account may have been embroidered slightly for visitors, but the tree is certainly gnarled, and does look of considerable age.

As mentioned above, the black mulberry is generally found as an individual specimen. In the United Kingdom, mulberry trees are usually isolated and some appear to be very old, including the one at Syon Park, which was apparently planted in 1548. However, on occasion trees have been planted in groups or avenues. For example, there is a mulberry avenue in the private gardens at Home Farm on the Windsor Castle estate that is thought to have been planted in the reign of Queen Victoria. A similar avenue was evident in the town of Rye in East Sussex but it no longer exists. Bonham Bazeley suggests that Queen Elizabeth I made an attempt to introduce mulberry trees for Flemish weavers at Rye, Sandwich and other sites along the south coast.[33] A portrait by Nicholas Hilliard (1547–1619), *c.*1575, in the collections of the Walker Art Gallery, shows Elizabeth I in sumptuous costume – she was obviously interested in promoting home-based textile production. There are groupings of trees at the St Fagans National History Museum in Cardiff (Survey List 21) and an orchard at Tiptree Farm, Colchester grown for jam makers Wilkin & Sons (Survey List 86). There is also a famous avenue of mulberry trees at Thomas Jefferson's (1743–1826) Monticello plantation in Virginia.[34]

Mulberry Survey

The intention of this study was to survey historic houses in England and Wales in order to establish the location of mulberry trees in general and more specifically those with attached histories and of significant age. The World Wide Web has various sites that list the location of mulberry trees in the United Kingdom and Ireland, including www.mulberrytrees. co.uk, which illustrates areas with a rich heritage of mulberry tree growth.[35] The website features a map centred on Bristol, pinpointing trees of varying ages, including examples in the University of Bristol Botanic Garden and Bath Botanical Gardens (apparently labelled sixteenth century).

The mulberry survey for this book was started in 2003 and completed in 2010. The survey material was posted to the recipients during the summer months in June, July and early August. The cohort for the survey was selected using the famous guide to historic homes and gardens produced by Hudsons.[36] This gives summary information on properties including their age and also a contact address and telephone number. Houses were selected if they were of apparent age, and priority was given to properties that were described as Tudor, Elizabethan or Jacobean. Enquiries were posted with an initial request for information in the form of a simple questionnaire, with questions pertaining to species, age, locality and use. Two envelopes were provided: a stamped, addressed reply envelope, and one for a sample leaf (to check for a positive identification).

After a final count, some 550 properties were sampled and there was a relatively good response rate (78%), with only 120 failing to respond. Of those that responded, 257 proved positive for *Morus* species while 173 proved negative. The rarest *Morus* species in the survey was *Morus rubra*, with only two identified. This is not surprising given that the red mulberry is in the main associated with North America, where items are occasionally made from the wood. The most common tree was *Morus nigra*, which was identified in 237 cases; various ages were identified, from under ten years to over 200 years old. These are detailed later,

with specific reference to various locations and the trees' attached histories. In a small number of cases, *Morus alba* was identified, with some relatively old examples. The specimen from Oxford University Botanic Garden (Survey List 51) is over 200 years old and has a typical *Morus* form, while the pendula species found at Wightwick Manor (Survey List 93) is not as old but is an impressive 'weeping' tree. A similar tree exists at Bodelwyddan, which features in the next chapter. In some cases (79 in total), the owner or gardener did not have a precise identification and the samples were labelled simply as *Morus* species. In all cases the owners/gardeners were asked to estimate the age of the trees. Sometimes this was done via actual records while in other cases the date could only be approximated. Black mulberry trees are difficult to date because they generally look older than they actually are. A tree specialist reported in 2002 on a very old collapsed mulberry tree at Chester Old Hall near Chester. He used dendrochronology, which simply involved counting the annual rings, and estimated that the tree was between 200 and 250 years old, but it did look older and was reported to have been planted in the reign of James I. The tree at East Bergholt Place (Survey List 40) has featured in dendrochronology literature even though it is only slightly over 100 years old. However, the tree does look ancient and is a good example of premature aging in a tree. Moreover, the tree fruits very well and this was evidenced in a photograph provided during the survey. Sadly, some mulberry trees died during the process of completing the survey and one such example has been included (Survey List 9). During rebuilding work at the Priest's House Museum, in Wimborne Minster, the 250-year-old mulberry had to be felled, despite efforts to replant it.

Once the initial survey material was returned, a further request was sent with a disposable camera. In every case the cameras were returned for processing and photographic development. Many interesting pieces of information were gathered and trees within the final sample can be classified into various groups, which are mainly related to the property and location. A guidebook was requested from all properties and gardens featured in Survey List and this constituted the main source of information in addition to the questionnaire. Further referenced texts and actual visits augmented this information and in some cases substantial amounts of material were sent by the recipients of the survey.

Gardens and Homes

The most common locality for mulberry trees in the United Kingdom is the garden and these are often attached to historic properties. Sometimes because of the importance of the landscape the gardens become more significant than the associated building. This is certainly the case with both Holehird Gardens (Survey List 70) and the Roof Gardens in Kensington (Survey List 79). The gardens at Holehird are tended by the Lakeland Horticultural Society and are located on a hilly site on the banks of Lake Windermere in Cumbria. The black mulberry there is at least 100 years old and is a relatively good specimen given its location – being on its northern limit and in an exposed area. This black mulberry is not the only altitude-placed mulberry in the United Kingdom as the one located off Kensington High Street, London (access via Derry Street) is six storeys up from the pavement and was planted as part of a roof garden designed by landscape designer Ralph Hancock (1859–1943), who was also responsible for the roof landscapes in the Rockefeller Center, New York.[37] The Kensington Roof Gardens are composed of Spanish-, Tudor- and English-themed areas, all designed by Hancock for Trevor Bowen, who managed the department store Derry and Toms that was located underneath the gardens. Hancock's designs were laid out between 1936 and 1938, with photographic evidence indicating that the gardens were quite skeletal when compared with the contemporary luxuriant growth. In 1976, Kensington and Chelsea Council placed a tree preservation order on the trees growing in the gardens to ensure that unnecessary removal or harmful pruning were not carried out, and importantly the gardens were eventually listed as a Grade II site in 1978 (English Heritage). The mulberry is documented as being part of the English woodland garden original planting list, so it is now over 70 years old and blends in with the other specimen trees, including various oaks, medlar and apple. Some of the trees are over 10 metres high and survive on less than 1 metre of substrata. A stream runs through the garden and after a restoration project instigated in 2007 by Richard Branson this now looks quite naturalistic and authentic, thanks in part to the efforts of the head gardener, David Lewis. Through a round 'window' or gap in the wall around the woodland site there are panoramic views across London – a bizarre juxtaposition between the rural and urban. This is probably the most unusual site for a mulberry tree in the country.

Many of the gardens included in the study are essentially landscaped into planned and designed man-made environments, and examples exist at Painswick (Survey List 15) and Painshill (Survey List 18). These both contain significant black mulberry trees in terms of size and age. Mapperton (Survey List 24) is listed Grade II* and its black mulberry is over 100 years old. The trees at Upton (Survey List 30) are in the care of the National Trust, with various black mulberry trees being planted in both the garden and orchard, while an older mulberry of significant age died in 2006. Humphry Repton (1752–1818) played a role in the design of gardens at certain localities, including Antony House (Survey List 39) and Longner Hall (Survey List 78). A considerable number of black mulberries are cared for by the National Trust and some trees have very picturesque settings, such as those at Dudmaston (Survey List 41) and Cliveden (Survey List 63), both of which have black mulberry trees that are over 150 years old. Perhaps one of the most lavish and perfectly recorded properties is Waddesdon Manor (Survey List 85): the black mulberry tree on the site can be accurately dated because there is a planting record and the tree was planted in 1874 within grounds which are now composed of formal areas and some significant topiary. There is no better example of topiary in Europe than the gardens at Levens Hall (Survey List 89). The black mulberry trees located within the grounds of this Elizabethan property look considerably older than they are in reality, the oldest being only approximately 50 years old. The age of the tree is clearly not always commensurate with the age of the property. Finally in this chapter, the garden at Iford Manor designed by the landscape architect Harold Peto (1854–1933) is of interest because it contains both a black mulberry tree (Survey List 12) and also a Japanese garden. These will be briefly discussed in Chapter 4.

The private homes included in the survey came via recommendation from people involved in the initial questionnaire – over twenty mulberry trees were suggested in this way. There was a high proportion of rectories (for example, Survey List 31) and seven sites were actually named after the mulberry in their garden, being called either Mulberry House or The Mulberries. A black mulberry in the garden of Mulberry House, in Withernsea, East Yorkshire, was not included in the photographic sample but it is interesting because it appears to be located very near to the sea and obviously survives in quite difficult conditions. This is contrary to general opinion that indicates that mulberries are sensitive to harsh climatic conditions. In a letter, the owner states: 'We are only 250 yards from the North Sea and consequently [the tree] is very one sided, i.e. nearly vertical on the sea side spreading out and branches touching the ground on the landward side.'[38]

A house called The Mulberries in Lewes, Sussex was not included in the final survey but did have an interesting history, and its tree was thought to be in place when John de la Chambre purchased the property in 1586 – making the tree over 400 years old. Those private residences that are featured in the Survey List include a mulberry in Hayton (Survey List 54) that was selected for inclusion because it is one of the furthest north in the United Kingdom, being only approximately 10 miles from the Scottish border. The black mulberry at Mulberry House at Pakenham, Suffolk (Survey List 84) is considered to be about 250 years old, while the magnificent black mulberry tree at Tower House, Wells was documented as being in place in 1794, making it over 200 years old (Survey List 66). This property was once owned by Elizabeth de Beauchamp Goudge, who included mention of the tree in her autobiography, *The Joy of the Snow*.[39] The present owner in a handwritten letter stated that originally two trees stood side by side and that one fell over in 1992 on an apparently quiet July day. The letter also mentions a memorial black mulberry tree being planted for the writer's deceased husband in the grounds of Wells Cathedral garden, and another tree at Wells in the Bishop's Palace gardens is Survey List 45. Because mulberry trees have a reputation for longevity they tend to be planted as memorial trees and, interestingly, the wood is also used for *memento mori* (see Chapter 5). Sometimes mulberry trees located in private residences can have resonance for owners who may not have a family attachment to the tree, as is the case with Dovenby Hall. This property is located in Cumbria (it is a few miles northwest of Cockermouth), which is quite far north for a mulberry to be entirely happy. However, the black mulberry tree is protected by a south-facing wall and was apparently grown from a truncheon taken by the Dykes family (around 1791) from the original tree which was at their family home at Warthole. There is an associated story passed from generation to generation which says that Thomas Dykes hid in the tree when Cromwell's men came to arrest him at the old family residence at Warthole. He was a devoted royalist and was eventually imprisoned at Cockermouth Castle because of his loyalty to the crown. The family motto is *Prius frangitur quam flectitur*, which roughly translates as 'You may sooner break than bend me.' The Dykes family gave up the hall in 1930 when it became a hospital. In 1998 it went into private ownership and was restored to a residence, office space and car workshop owned by Malcolm Wilson and used for M-Sport – the Ford Rally Team. The mulberry tree is still on the site.

The black mulberry tree located in Chipping Campden (Survey List 62) was at one time a tourist attraction and open for public viewing – now it is in private ownership in the High Street of the Cotswold village. The tree is of considerable age and is a beautifully shaped tree in what is a typical cottage garden location. The tree was recorded as being planted in 1702 and was possibly grown (in part) for the leaves which could have been used for a nascent silk industry. The silk mill at Chipping Campden was established in 1710 and was mainly responsible for the creation of silk fibre for the textile industry. The factory ceased production by 1859 due to high-quality imports.[40] There are other locations in the United Kingdom that still produce silk, including Sudbury in Suffolk, which has the Gainsborough Silk Weaving Company.[41] There is also a magnificent mulberry tree in the gardens of Gainsborough's House, which was the home of the landscape and portrait painter Thomas Gainsborough (1727–1788). It states on the website:

> The Gainsborough's House mulberry tree is spectacular with its spreading, giant boughs now propped by tree stumps, [which] still produce a fine crop of fruit. The silkworm breeding industry did not take off, thanks in part to the lack of botanical knowledge of the King and his advisers. There are two kinds of mulberry tree – the white, which feeds silkworms, and the black, which supplies fruit. It is the black mulberry tree that was cultivated in England, in estates and substantial gardens throughout the country.[42]

Country Life and Stately Home

Certain properties have mulberry trees that could be described as having an Arts and Crafts heritage. Mulberry trees have always been associated with Englishness, to such an extent that Roger Saul decided to name his heritage-fashion- based company after the tree (this is discussed further in Chapter 2). The Arts and

Crafts movement is also identified as particularly English and it is not surprising that the mulberry tree should be found in so many Arts and Crafts gardens. The Arts and Crafts tradition has often been associated with nature and the naturalistic[43] and the Arts and Crafts home nearly always has an important garden associated with the property. In certain instances there are also famous gardeners associated with the site. This is certainly the case with Great Dixter, which had a house and garden redesigned by Sir Edwin Lutyens (1869–1944). In many of his house/garden designs he collaborated with the garden designer Gertrude Jekyll (1843–1932), but, surprisingly, in Great Dixter's case (given its aesthetic), Lutyens completed the designs on his own. The famous gardener associated with Great Dixter is Christopher Lloyd (1921–2006), who developed the design throughout the twentieth century and wrote the guide to the gardens. Great Dixter appeared in *Country Life* in 1913 and then again in 1995.[44] Its black mulberry tree (Survey List 34) is over 90 years old and is located by the Long Border, which is near the terrace of the property, and you can move from the mulberry to the orchard. The gardens, which wrap around the property, maintain the Lutyens masterplan and are quintessentially English, with orchards, moats, topiary, wild flower meadows, lawns and an oast house. The planting features mixed borders with traditional cottage garden plants and well-established trees, including pears and fig. Not surprisingly, the mulberry trees associated with Arts and Crafts properties are not always of considerable age, and this is the case with Rodmarton Manor (Survey List 83), Standen (Survey List 98) and also Wightwick Manor (Survey List 93). The exception is Kelmscott Manor, the home of William Morris (1834–1896). Unlike the Red House, in Bexleyheath, Kelmscott was an old and established property when Morris moved in and the black mulberry is a magnificent specimen that is around 200 years old (Survey List 1). The whole house and its history are featured in the book *William Morris's Kelmscott Landscape and History*,[45] and this will be detailed more comprehensively in Chapter 5.

While the Arts and Crafts movement fostered traditional craft heritage and established the aesthetic values of the medieval guilds, the following group of houses and gardens captures the true essence of heritage and history.[46] It was always the original purpose of the mulberry survey to focus on properties built or in place during the reign of James I in the hope that old mulberry trees could be recorded. Indeed, there are over 30 included in the Survey List, from relatively small manor houses such as Canons Ashby (Survey List 44) to Burghley House – an Elizabethan palace (Survey List 59). These houses include examples that can be described as Tudor, Elizabethan or Jacobean and include many Grade I listed buildings. Most of the gardens are of major cultural significance, including those at the halls (Survey List 5, 25, 43, 53), houses (Survey List 8, 10, 22, 23, 32, 58, 59, 97), courts (Survey List 47, 95), castles (Survey List 2, 4, 26, 38, 42, 68) and manors (Survey List 16). The black mulberry trees are of varying ages but tend to be very old – for example, the tree at Hellens is 320 years old (Survey List 28), the specimen at Quenby Hall (Survey List 5) is 300 years old and the mulberry at Charlecote Park (Survey List 13) is 250 years old. Some of the trees are in good health (for example, the 400-year-old tree at Temple Newsam House – Survey List 97), though it appears that others are not in good condition, such as the 300-year-old tree at Breamore House (Survey List 22), which is obviously in poor health.

There is a selection of properties which have associations with the Royal Family, including Burghley House (Survey List 59), which was owned by William Cecil (1520–1598), and Hatfield House (Survey List 32), which Robert Cecil acquired in 1607. This remains the seat of the Cecil family and has a remarkable picture of Elizabeth I – *The Rainbow Portrait c*.1600, by Isaac Oliver (1595–1617), who was a pupil of Hilliard. The picture is infused with symbolism, the cloth being decorated with eyes and ears implying that the queen sees and hears all. Sudeley Castle (Survey List 4) has direct connections with two of Henry VIII's wives – Jane Seymour (1509–1537) and Katherine Parr (1512–1548) – while Hever Castle (Survey List 38) has associations with both Anne of Cleves (1515–1557) and Anne Boleyn (1501–1536).[47] Thus, the connection between the Royal Family and mulberry trees has passed through history to the present day and the national collection.

Most of the properties are cared for as stately homes and can be visited by the public, and the National Trust has an impressive portfolio of buildings, including what is probably the jewel in the crown of the Elizabethan period – Hardwick Hall (Survey List 43). This property has featured in a DVD collection produced by the National Trust entitled *National Trust National Treasures*.[48] The property has also featured in *World of Interiors*, with multiple illustrations of the textiles, plasterwork ceilings and tapestries.[49] The hall has been restored

and kept in fine condition and the gardens have a collection of mulberry trees, some of which have been planted in recent years. The hall was constructed during the 1590s by Bess of Hardwick (1521–1608) and had far larger windows than was the norm (more glass than wall) and a classical entrance colonnade. The interiors are sumptuous and contain many finely embroidered fabrics and hangings in the state rooms; its textiles will be discussed in Chapter 2. Bess had hopes of a royal visit from Elizabeth I on one of her progresses, but this never happened. The interior sequence of rooms was arranged in a similar way to a royal palace and the iconography was akin to royal arms and insignia. Bess had her initials and coronets emblazoned within the strapwork on top of the perfectly symmetrical building.

Another interesting property that has a relatively old black mulberry is Eltham Palace (Survey List 67), which also has a connection with the Mulberry company because Mulberry was responsible for producing contemporary fabrics for the house (such as a cream Maze Matelasse).[50] The guidebook states:

> The decorative schemes and furnishings on display are, to a large extent, reproductions by English Heritage. They have been accurately recreated on the evidence of archive material and photographs to give an impression of the interior's appearance in the Courtaulds' time and English Heritage acknowledges Mulberry Home for the sponsorship of textiles for Eltham Palace.

The property is interesting in the fact that it is juxtaposed between the very old Great Hall and 1933 moderne, including the use of concrete and contemporary finishes and fixings. It was famously owned by the Courtauld family who had a very successful business making artificial silk (Rayon). Stephen Courtauld (1883–1967) and his wife Virginia became famous for their extravagant, philanthropic and avant-garde lifestyle (they had a pet ring-tailed lemur that lived in the house). The designers Rolf Engstromer (1892–1970) and Peter Malacrida (1889–1980) were responsible for much of the interior work alongside many notable craftspeople, artists and artisans. The property featured in *Country Life* over three editions in 1937.[51]

Education and Religion

There are a number of black mulberry trees associated with the colleges at both Oxford and Cambridge universities, some of significant age and in beautiful settings. The most famous, at Christ's College, Cambridge (Survey List 7), has been mentioned previously and will be considered further in Chapter 5. The college has a long history, being established in 1505, while the black mulberry within the grounds of Pembroke College, Cambridge was recorded in an engraving by David Logan (1635–1700?) as a large tree in the 1680s and has been regenerated on at least one occasion. It was originally thought to have come from a churchyard (Survey List 72). Other colleges in Cambridge have various black mulberry trees, including St John's College, which has three – one of which is very old – with two additional younger specimens.

The most perfect mulberry in terms of location, shape, condition and fruiting is that at Merton College, Oxford (Survey List 100). The college was founded in 1264 and overlooks Christ Church meadows and the Thames to the south. The college has some significant and old trees but the oldest is the black mulberry tree which was established during the reign of James I and was almost certainly planted by Sir Henry Saville (warden of Merton 1585–1622). There is also a younger tree that was planted during the 1950s and that was nearly lost in the 1980s when it split in half because of the weight of the fruit. The tree was bolted and cabled and still survives. Further educational links appear at Winchester College, which has a number of mulberry trees associated with medlar, apple, walnut and almond trees; the oldest tree is thought to be aged over 100 and is harvested for fruit that is used in the college kitchens (Survey List 56).

The mulberry at Carshalton (Survey List 49) is now located within school grounds. Perhaps the most interesting educational location is one that would not at first be suspected of having much history. However, the tree at Exeter Community Centre (Survey List 64) is noteworthy because the old black mulberry tree is on the site of a silk merchant's house. A letter from the centre states that as far back as anyone living can remember the tree was being propped up by steel supports and had to be cut back in the 1980s. During the 1960s, the centre was a school for the blind. In the letter, Julie Bennett comments: 'The community centre was until the 1960s "the West of England School for Blind and Partially Sighted Children." Before that a merchant's house formed the core of the site. Many former pupils of "W of E" school remember the tree.' She further writes: 'Many of the former pupils regard the tree as an important symbol of their time here, as do many of the former users of Exeter Community Centre.'[52] It is certainly true that people tend never to forget a mulberry tree, and in the course of this study numerous owners and gardeners reiterated their fondness and love of their mulberry trees.

John Feltwell's *The Story of Silk* has one chapter entitled 'Mulberries, Monasteries and Gardens', which is in the main devoted to religious sites, including monastery and cathedral gardens, vicarages, rectories and churchyards.[53] He writes: 'There is considerable evidence to support my original hunch that "men of the cloth" were in fact "men of the silk cloth". To me it was more than just coincidence that mulberry trees were all too frequently found in cathedral precincts, priories, churchyards, rectories, vicarages and abbeys.' It appears that both monks and priests could have originally used the trees for both food and drink (wine).

There is evidence that many counties have religious associations with mulberry trees, particularly Kent, but also Gloucestershire, Leicestershire, Lincolnshire, London, Somerset, Suffolk, Surrey, East/West Sussex and Warwickshire. There is a famous garden designed in the eighteenth century for Bishop Henry Ellacombe of Bitten in Gloucestershire which has a collection of exotic trees including mulberry. The bishop was a Shakespearean scholar and perhaps it is this connection that persuaded him to grow a mulberry like those in Stratford-upon-Avon. The complex story of Shakespeare and his mulberry trees will be featured in Chapter 5. In terms of this study, a significant number of old black mulberry trees have been documented in various cathedral grounds including Rochester (Survey List 29), Canterbury (Survey List 52), Chichester (Survey List 65), Peterborough (Survey List 76), Exeter (Survey List 87) and Winchester (Survey List 91). In addition, there are also trees associated with cathedral precincts or properties including Fulham Palace (Survey List 46), Archdeacons Lodging, Christ Church, Oxford (Survey List 50) and Deanery Garden, Winchester Cathedral (Survey List 94). Other cathedrals that are not included in the Survey List have mulberry trees, such as St Pauls, London, while others did have old trees that are no longer present, such as Chester Cathedral.

Some properties, such as Anglesey Abbey (Survey List 33), Buckland Abbey (Survey List 74), Torre Abbey (Survey List 75) and Walsingham Abbey (Survey List 90) have historic associations with various religious orders, including the Cistercians and Augustinians. Although these properties have a long and remarkable history, the mulberry trees associated with them tend not to be old, ranging from 50 years to 150 years of age. Feltwell indicates that mulberry trees were recorded as being present in monastic gardens around Canterbury in the twelfth century and York in the thirteenth century, so clearly they have a very long history of attachment to religious sites. Some have thought that the tree has religious significance because the juice of the fruit has been described as blood-like and symbolic of the blood of Christ. The leaves in the majority of cases have a heart shape, which may also be significant.

Law and Prison

Middle Temple Hall in London is one of the oldest of the Inns of Court and nearby is an open garden area called Fountains Court, which is off Middle Temple Lane. It is here that four mulberry trees were planted for Queen Victoria's Golden Jubilee (1887), although there are only two remaining, both of which are located near to a chestnut (Castanea sativa) and a laburnum (Laburnum anagyroides).[54] The hall and its environs have remained relatively unspoilt for over 400 years since the building was completed in 1573. Queen Elizabeth I (1533–1603) was both a benefactor and guest, and famous men having associations with the place include Sir Walter Raleigh (1552–1618) and Sir Francis Drake (1540–1596). The hall contains a magnificent window with the arms of Lord Chancellors, judges and members of Middle Temple. It survived the Great Fire of London (1666) and the Second World War (1939–1945) and is still central to the lawyers who use it on a daily basis. Fountains Court was restored to celebrate the millennium in 2000, including the introduction of new paving, railings and lighting, with a fountain in the middle of the development (Survey List 99).

Wakefield Prison was founded as a House of Correction in around 1595 and a significant building was in place by 1611, which was run by the Justices of West Riding, Yorkshire.[55] The institution was apparently in its early years open to men, women and also children. The original building has evolved and the prison was rapidly expanded in the Victorian period; much of the Victorian wings remain today. It is a very bleak place and houses maximum-security prisoners, many serving life sentences. Two black mulberry trees were thought to have been planted in 1632 and the prison claims that the nursery rhyme 'Here We Go Round the Mulberry Bush' was sung by women and children in the House of Correction as they exercised around the trees. One of the trees was relocated outside the prison boundary while the one left in the prison has had a preservation order placed on it. The tree is virtually the only piece of nature within the prison environs and actually does look more like a bush than a tree. As part of their rehabilitation process the prisoners make small mementos out of surplus wood from pruning, such as key fobs (Illustration 4) and pens. These have an attached Certificate of Authenticity which is signed by the governor.

Conclusion

This chapter has focused mainly on the geography of the mulberry tree, giving some indication of the spread of trees throughout England and Wales. At the present time the areas that have the greatest number of trees are the Home Counties around London and Kent, though other areas also have significant mulberry presence, including the Cotswolds, Cumbria and the south coast with Devon and Cornwall. Bochym Manor, Cury, Cornwall apparently has a mulberry tree over 1,000 years old but this is unconfirmed. Another significant area is around Bath, including trees that have not been photographed for the survey – for example, the National Trust property Dyrham Park, which has a 150-year-old black mulberry tree. The house contains an unusual artefact which uses mulberry – the inventory indicates a pair of seventeenth-century holster pistols with mulberry wood stocks. Probably because of the rarity of mulberry wood, no other properties featured in the survey and questionnaire identified any items made out of the wood in their collections.

Jules David Prown, in his article 'Mind in Matter', writes: 'The most essential quality of an object for the study of material culture, after survival, is authenticity. The optimum object is the gravestone because it is geographically rooted and attended by a great deal of primary data.'[56] The same could be said of mulberry trees in that they are rooted in the landscape (usually by permanent architecture) and often have data which can detail their age, reasons for planting and usage. The history attached to the trees can be very complex and convoluted, being based on folklore, storytelling and actual fact. Sometimes the owners of trees have been very fastidious in making a record, and a tree book by the Massingberd family exists at Gunby Hall (Survey List 81) which dates from 1670. The geography is far more straightforward because apart from slight movement of trees they are fixed geographically in a high proportion of cases. The survey has given an overview of 'change over space' in that it indicates the spaces which mulberry trees inhabit. In later chapters, items, whether produced directly in textile and wood, or via imagery of the trees, will be detailed. Often these objects have been produced after the death of the tree through natural or man-made circumstances. It is these objects that give the mulberry tree even more longevity and root the tree firmly within our material culture.

Notes to Chapter 1

1   Jenny Linford, *A Concise Guide to Trees* (Bicester: Baker and Taylor, 2009). Trees are also featured in a series of programmes entitled *The Secret Power of Trees* for BBC Radio 4, first broadcast in 2012. In the promotional material it states: 'With the rise of "social forestry", woodlands have come to be seen as therapeutic and healing, and not just by New Age eco types. In Japan, doctors take seriously the practice of "forest air bathing", and claim all kinds of health benefits from simply being in the woods'. See 'A Collection of Programmes Devoted to Trees': www.bbc.co.uk/programmes/p012czgd (accessed 23 May 2015).

2   *Deep Rooted: How Trees Shape Our Lives*, exhibition pamphlet produced by the Whitworth Art Gallery, Manchester (2010). The exhibition ran from 1 August 2009 to 31 May 2010.

3   Mary Schoeser, *Silk* (New Haven, Conn.: Yale University Press, 2007), with reference to the chapter 'Sericulture' by Silvio Farago and specifically the section 'Silk in History' (pp. 60–65).

4   Adam Bowett, *Woods in British Furniture Making, 1400–1900 (An Illustrated Historical Dictionary)* (Wetherby: Oblong Creative Ltd, 2012). This features information on both black and white mulberry wood and its use (pp. 157–159), including illustrations of a very rare mulberry table *c.*1690 (p. 158) and a tea caddy by George Cowper *c.*1760 (p. 159).

5   Correspondence dated 25 August 2005 to the author from Mr D. E. Thornber (Arboricultural Officer, West Lancashire District Council Tree Section).

6   Correspondence dated 1 August 2005 to the author from Dominic Blake (Landscape and Arboricultural Manager, Royal Kingston Council).

7   'Ancient Tree Lives on as Memorial to New Nation', *East Anglia District Times*, 25 June 1993, p. 47.

8   'Milton's Mulberry', episode 5 (of 8), of *Meetings with Remarkable Trees*, BBC4 television programme, series 2, presented by Thomas Pakenham and first broadcast in 2008. The series had an accompanying book, *Meetings with Remarkable Trees* (London: Weidenfeld & Nicolson, 1996), with text and photographs by Thomas Pakenham, which does not contain information on the Milton mulberry tree. An abridged audiobook version, produced by Orion and read by Bill Paterson, was published in 2000.

9   Bonham Bazeley, 'Royal Mulberries', *The Garden*, June 1992, p. 286.

10 Jo Stokes and Donald Rodger, *Heritage Trees of Britain and Northern Island* (London: Constable, 2004), p. 115.

11 'Charlton House, Kent, Seat of Sir Spencer P. Maryon-Wilson', *Country Life*, 1 May 1909, pp. 630–638, and 8 May 1909, pp. 666–676. Cited in Beverley Burford, *Images of Charlton House: A Pictorial History* (London: Greenwich Council, 2002).

12 The information was provided by Lullingstone Castle, Eynsford, Kent. The property is now part managed by Tom Dyke Hart and he has developed a world garden that has featured in print and on television.

13 Private correspondence from Mark Lane (Gardens Manager), stamped 'Property Section Buckingham Palace' and dated 8 September 2003. He is also quoted in Yvonne Thomas, 'The Fruit of Queens', *Daily Telegraph*, 31 May 2003, in the Gardening section (p. 3), where she mentions that blackbirds love mulberry fruit.

14 Dan Pearson, 'Round the Mulberry Bush', *Observer Magazine*, 27 August 2006, pp. 52 and 55.

15 See https://www.rickstein.com/about/rick-stein/ricks-tv-travels/food-heroes/ (accessed 21 September 2012).

16 Interview by Tamsin Blanchard, 'Nigel Slater's Garden of Earthly Delights', *Daily Telegraph*, 26 September 2009, www.telegraph.co.uk/foodanddrink/6222663/Nigel-Slater-recipes-garden-of-earthly-delights.html (accessed 17 August 2012).

17 Recipe posted by chaitanya, www.nigella.com/recipes/view/mulberry-sauce-4486 (accessed 16 August 2012).

18 *The Great British Bake Off*, episode 5, first broadcast on BBC2 television in 2013; produced by Love Productions and directed by Scott Tankard, featuring Paul Hollywood, Mary Berry, Sue Perkins and Mel Giedroyc. The programme featured a piece on a tray bake, called Tottenham Cake, originated around 1901 by Henry Chalkley. Chalkley was a Quaker who had access to the grounds of the Tottenham Meeting House in which there was a mulberry tree. The fruit was harvested for the juice, which was an ingredient in the pink icing on top of the cake. The tradition of making the cake is continued by the Friends.

19 Peter Blackburne-Maze, *Fruit: An Illustrated History* (London: Scriptum Editions, in association with the Royal Horticultural Society, 2003).

20 John Feltwell, *The Story of Silk* (Stroud: Alan Sutton Publishing, 1990).

21 Blackburne-Maze, *Fruit*, p. 115.

22 The various livery companies and their treasures are featured in Clive Aslet, 'Are the Streets Still Paved with Gold?', *Country Life*, 12–19 December 2012, pp. 128–132.

23 Archive material from Drapers' Hall: Arboricultural Consultancy Service correspondence dated 8 November 2000 to Mrs Vincent from R. D. D. Grainger. For a comprehensive history of Drapers' Hall, see Penelope Hunting, *A History of The Drapers' Company* (London: Drapers' Company, 1989).

24 Private correspondence dated 23 June 2005 to the author from Diane Davis (Bank of England Public Information and Enquiries Group).

25 Feltwell, *The Story of Silk*.

26 Research information notes in a letter dated 24 May 2008 from Royal Botanic Garden Edinburgh.

27 G. Koidzumi, 'Taxonomy and Phytogeography of the Genus *Morus*', *Bulletin of Sericultural Experimental Station* (Tokyo), 3 (1917), pp. 1–62.

28 K. Vijayan, 'Genetic Relationships of Japanese and Indian Mulberry (*Morus* spp.) Genotypes Revealed by DNA Fingerprinting', *Plant Systematics and Evolution*, 243 (2004), pp. 221–232.

29 Feltwell, *The Story of Silk*, p. 75.

30 Ibid.

31 Rose Prince, 'Save the Vauxhall Two', *Daily Telegraph*, 26 February 2011, p. 24.

32 General website for gardening information and advice, www.telegraph.co.uk/gardening (accessed 20 September 2012).

33 Bonham Bazeley, 'Royal Mulberries', *The Garden*, June 1992, pp. 284–286.

34 Frederick D. Nichols and James A. Bear, Jr, *Monticello: A Guidebook* (Charlottesville, Va.: Thomas Jefferson Memorial Foundation, 1993).

35 www.mulberrytrees.co.uk (accessed 20 May 2012) is a website containing much general information

about mulberry trees and their location in the United Kingdom.

36 *Hudson's Historic Houses and Gardens, Castles and Heritage Sites* (Banbury: Norman Hudson & Co., 2003).

37 See www.ralphhancock.com, including pages: 'The Roof Gardens at Derry and Toms' and 'Kensington Roof Gardens Reborn' (accessed 22 August 2012).

38 Private correspondence dated 25 April 2008 to the author from Frank Swain of Withernsea, East Yorkshire.

39 Elizabeth Goudge, *The Joy of the Snow* (New York: Coward, McCann & Geoghegan, 1974). Mulberry trees are mentioned on p. 79 and also in the chapter 'The Family of the Silk Weaver' (p. 101).

40 Catherine Gordon, *Chipping Campden (Towns and Villages of England)* (Stroud: Alan Sutton Publishing, 1993).

41 Diane Sargeant, 'A Secret History of Taste: Gainsborough Silk Mill', *Journal for Weavers, Spinners and Dyers*, 239 (2011), pp. 24–27.

42 See www.gainsborough.org/page/479/Garden (accessed 25 October 2012).

43 Anna Jackson, *The V&A Guide to Period Styles: 400 Years of British Art and Design* (London: V&A Publications, 2006).

44 A number of images of Great Dixter are featured on the *Country Life* website: www.countrylifeimages.co.uk. See the black-and-white photograph of the south side (Image Number 959375) from the 4 January 1913 issue (p. 18) and the colour photograph (by Paul Barker) of the east front of the house and garden (Image Number 740556) from 2 November 1995 (p. 50).

45 Alan Crossley, Tom Hassall and Peter Salway (eds), *William Morris's Kelmscott Landscape and History* (Macclesfield: Windgather Press, 2007).

46 Michael Snodin and John Styles, *Design and the Decorative Arts: Tudor and Stuart Britain, 1500–1714* (London: V&A Publications, 2004).

47 For an excellent context to the court of Henry VIII (1491–1547), Thomas Cromwell (1485–1540) and the downfall of Anne Boleyn, see the first two Booker-prize-winning books of Hilary Mantel's trilogy, *Wolf Hall* (London: Fourth Estate, 2009) and *Bring up the Bodies* (London: Fourth Estate, 2012). In *Wolf Hall*

there is mention of More's mulberry trees. Mantel cites Shakespeare as an early source of inspiration: see 'Hilary Mantel Discusses Thomas Cromwell's Past, Presence and Future', *Guardian*, 15 August 2012: www.theguardian.com/books/2012/aug/15/hilary-mantel-edinburgh-wolf-hall (accessed 20 October 2012).

48 *National Trust National Treasures*, Jon Woods (dir.) (2008). DVD set of ten discs, produced in collaboration with SkyARTS, and including Hardwick Hall and Bateman's.

49 Mark Girouard, 'The Derbyshire Dowagers', *World of Interiors*, 28.11 (2008), pp. 120–131.

50 Roger Saul, *Mulberry at Home* (London: Ebury Press, 1999).

51 Christopher Hussey, 'Eltham Hall', *Country Life*, 15 May 1937, pp. 534–539; 22 May 1937, pp. 568–573; 29 May 1937, pp. 594–599. The property also featured in a BBC television programme, *Britain's Hidden Heritage*, broadcast in 2012, with presenter Clare Balding visiting both the *Country Life* head offices and Eltham Palace and filmed in conversation with English Heritage curator Annie Kemkaran Smith. Another residence, called Mulberry House, at Smith Square, Westminster, designed in 1911 by Sir Edwin Lutyens, appeared in *Country Life* (6 June 1931, pp. 736–738) after an Art Deco redesign by Darcy Braddell, and was the home of the scandalous Mond family (Henry and Gwen).

52 Private correspondence (no date) handwritten by Julie Bennett from the Exeter Community Centre as part of the survey material returned with leaves and camera.

53 Feltwell, *The Story of Silk*, specifically the chapter 'Mulberries, Monasteries and Gardens' (pp. 100–112), p. 100.

54 Information received from a letter dated 6 July 2005 to the author from I. M. Garwood (Director of Estates). This included an information pack with plans, maps and photographs.

55 'Here we go around the Mulberry Bush: The House of Correction 1595', in R. S. Duncan, *The West Riding House of Correction and H.M. Prison Wakefield* (Wakefield: Wakefield Print & Design, 1995).

56 Jules David Prown, 'Mind in Matter: An Introduction to Material Culture Theory and Method', *Winterthur Portfolio*, 17.1 (1982), pp. 1–19, in the section 'Modifications of the Landscape' (pp. 13–14), p. 13.

2

Change over Time

Introduction

In the book to accompany the exhibition *Perspectives on the Decorative Arts of Early America*, which was held at the Winterthur Museum and opened in the Winterthur Galleries in 1992, it states in the section 'Change over Time': 'Designs and purposes of all kinds of objects change over time, and the reasons that certain objects or features appear, change, and disappear are as complex as the human forces that originally created them ... Among the many reasons for change is fashion.'[1] In this chapter, the objects influenced by mulberry trees via imagery and style will be dealt with, from the contemporary to the old. The well-known and successful fashion brand Mulberry has already been very briefly mentioned but the history of their heritage brand and the story of how a mulberry tree found its way to the space outside their headquarters merits telling in greater detail. The company has been in the news in recent years because of its drive to retain and expand its manufacturing base in the United Kingdom. On its website it states:

> Mulberry is proud to be the only luxury brand retaining and investing in its UK factory. In 2006 Mulberry launched an apprenticeship scheme in the UK factory, sustaining a way of working that has lasted generations and providing skills,

training, and employment for the local community. The Mulberry customer appreciates superior quality, fashion-forward design, and understated luxury.[2]

In order to ascertain details of the company and how it became established, Roger Saul, the founder, was asked to write a history of the company from his own perspective. The following is taken directly from his letter:

> – I am sending you a short history of Mulberry (to 1980) but in brief:
>
> – The name came out of a hat. We did not want to use Roger Saul because all the successful accessory designers were French or Italian at the time, e.g. Yves Saint Laurent, Pierre Cardin etc., so we chose a very English name almost as a bold statement.
>
> – The Mulberry harbour was designed by the Admiralty at my school, Kingswood, in Bath. They had requisitioned it for the duration so that came to mind and also that it was a great provider, wood, fruit, etc.
>
> – My sister was a graphic designer and we asked her to design a very modern image to demonstrate

design and modernity beside the Mulberry brand name which we felt was very traditional and showed longevity.

– I started the company with my mother in 1971 with £500 capital.[3]

Further details were provided concerning the early history of Mulberry – essentially the company was developed via a present of some money for Roger's twenty-first birthday. He had joined John Michael (a retailer in Carnaby Street, London) as an assistant and considered branching out on his own and decided to concentrate on leather goods. He asked his father (a senior manager at a shoe company) where to buy equipment, etc. for small-scale production and he started manufacturing snakeskin chokers in 1969/70. They proved a success and he sold his range to many fashion retailers such as BIBA (in the Derry and Toms building). In addition to chokers he had also started designing leather belts, and this continued under the banner of Mulberry. Successful sales trips abroad meant that by the middle of the 1970s his exports were good and his home business was also thriving.

Some of the notable names selling his products included Christian Aujard, Henri Bendel, Fiorucci and Browns of London. In addition, Roger was also designing belts and handbags for various collections such as Kenzo, Ralph Lauren, Burberry and Jaeger. He also designed with more functional leathers taking inspiration from classic English saddlery and military styles. Some of his fashion collections proved incredibly successful and Mulberry was beginning to be associated with a classic anglophile look, including hunting-, shooting- and fishing-inspired items. He became part of the London Designer Collections and showed in London, Paris, Milan and New York. The first Mulberry shop was opened in Paris in 1980 on the Place des Victoires. The fashion empire became increasingly successful, even branching into giftware such as pens (Illustration 5) and golf accessories. This eventually evolved into homeware, with the creation of Mulberry Home with Jill Evans in 1991. There was also a hotel called Charlton House in Somerset (again a mulberry-themed name – see Chapter 1 for details of the Charlton House black mulberry tree) established in 1994 with Ian Jupp and a team including his wife, Monty. The brand continued to expand worldwide and particularly in Japan whilst also opening a shop in Manchester and a flagship Mulberry Home store on the Kings Road, London (which was later to become the Shaker shop). In the foreword to the book *Mulberry at Home*, David Bailey writes: 'Real taste is as rare as some rainforest orchids. Anyone can buy a certain kind of taste in Bond Street or find it in numerous magazines, yet true, individual taste cannot simply be bought ... Roger Saul has this individual taste.'[4]

The Mulberry Home company produced many varied and different collections, taking inspiration from a multitude of sources, including the Restoration period with fabrics such as Tudor Animals and Garden Plan (Illustration 6). The company used architectural heritage to create a quintessentially English style which has become associated with the same iconic mulberry tree logotype/brand as the fashion and accessory business (see Illustration 7). Sadly, Roger Saul was removed from the parent company in 2003 after a rather acrimonious period with board members, and some of this history is featured in an article by Louisa Peacock entitled 'Mulberry: From Somerset to Singapore'.[5] The Mulberry Home range, including fabrics and accessories, can now be found at Chelsea Harbour Design Centre (also under new ownership). In 2011, the company produced a book with numerous photographs celebrating its 40

5 English Mulberry company fountain pen

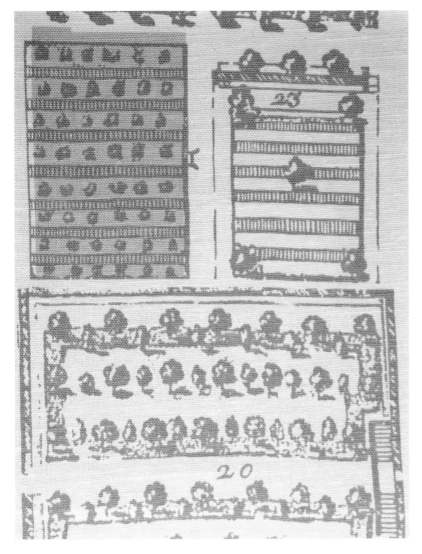

6 English fabric from Mulberry Home, called 'Secret Gardens'

part of a garden exhibit for the Chelsea Flower Show in 1994, designed by Julian and Isabel Bannerman (from Bristol) for the Telegraph Newspaper group and based around an old abbey garden. A description of the garden can be found in the Chelsea Flower Show catalogue for the event.[7] The tree was already thought to be at least 100 years old and was 8 metres high when it was chosen for the garden and was then moved on an articulated lorry to Chelsea by Ruskin's Tree Moving Ltd. The mulberry tree was originally on a site next to a property that had been demolished and was purchased from the owner of the land who was a farmer. The transportation of the tree was featured in an article in the *Weekend Telegraph*.[8] The root ball weighed six tons and the tree was clearly not in leaf when it was moved. Amazingly, given all the circumstances of the move, the tree did produce leaves and the garden won a gold medal from the judges. In the *Telegraph* article it states: 'the tree can look forward to a glamorous middle-age: its next home will be the garden of a certain leather-goods company's HQ, where it will stand as a living logo'. When it was at the Flower Show the mulberry tree could be described as ideal for the essentially English garden – in terms of both the design and planting. It was set into a lawn area and was surrounded by topiary, herbaceous borders, mature shrubs, roses and ferns. The architectural salvage was from Walcot Reclamation and also contained upcycled authentic ecclesiastical pieces from the restoration of Salisbury Cathedral.

The tree was in turn again repackaged and moved to Somerset to its current position (Illustration 8). A further article in the *Daily Telegraph* entitled 'Mulberry Moves On' stated: 'Weighing 10 tons, and with roots 12 ft across protected in a metal frame, it was lifted by crane onto a transporter vehicle yesterday and travelled down the M4 overnight. For the rest of the summer the tree will be watered automatically by a computerised system which will monitor readings from moisture probes buried in the soil.'[9] The move was obviously a success as the tree is growing well and is a healthy specimen.

years in the fashion industry. The mulberry tree logo has become part of the iconography of the world brand, reflecting tradition, heritage and design in leather and other materials. The association of the company with the mulberry tree has become fixed and permanent, with the symbol on every product and often quite visible – for example, on one tote bag it is over 10 cm across. It seems appropriate therefore that the company should have a real mulberry tree at its base in Somerset.

Mulberry plc and Mulberry sp
A black mulberry tree grows outside the headquarters of the Mulberry company in the village of Chilcompton, near Shepton Mallet, Somerset.[6] The tree is now well established but in actual fact it has not been at the site for very long – less than 20 years. The tree has an interesting history because, whilst mulberry trees have a reputation for wandering, this tree has moved many miles during its life. The tree was

Textiles, Colour and Scent
The Mulberry Home company still produces fabrics which are decorated with the mulberry tree motif; one example is called Orchard Linen which is a lightweight, machine-embroidered fabric specifically designed for window treatments. Other mulberry-inspired fabrics have been produced by various companies for

different functions in both interior and fashion sectors. A variety of textiles and decorative items have been associated with mulberry imagery including trees and leaves. Some have been created in design studios for companies such as Hermès, whilst others have used traditional sources as inspiration for contemporary designs. One such example is the fabric called Mulberry Trees (Illustration 9) produced for the company Fired Earth. As the name suggests, this company specialises in high-quality tiles and various fixtures for interiors. Because of its success it has expanded into other areas related to the interior, including furniture, paints and fabrics. The fabric Mulberry Trees is based on a seventeenth-century Flemish tapestry and was available in the early twenty-first century, but has now been discontinued. The cotton-based tapestry-like fabric shows realistic colour images of fruiting mulberry trees and could be purchased by the metre, with cushions and throws also available in the range. The company Morris & Co. has recently produced a richly embroidered fabric reminiscent of Elizabethan work called Kelmscott Tree, which is featured in Michael Parry's *Morris & Co.: A Revolution in Decoration*[10] and which could have been based on the mulberry tree at Kelmscott Manor (Survey List 1). The tree at Kelmscott is discussed in greater detail in Chapter 5.

A more contemporary mulberry referenced name (White Mulberry) has been introduced in a paint range for Fired Earth with colours formulated by Kevin McCloud. He is described by the company as a leading authority on colour and is associated with television and a focus on entertainment in the fields of interiors and architecture. The paint is widely available and the cream/white colour complements the other shades in the comprehensive range of 120 colours that can be viewed on a paint chart supplied by the company. Another high-end company, Molton Brown, also produce a range called Mulberry and Thyme which includes 'Air' room scents and hand treatments.

Embroidery – Twixt Art and Nature

Expanding on the Elizabethan/Jacobean textile theme, there are two objects displayed at the V&A which resonate in respect to the use of plants, fruit and vegetables in embroidered textile imagery. The V&A Guide Book, *British Galleries, 1500–1900*, in the section 'Dressing for Magnificence, 1600–1630' elaborates about a portrait and embroidered jacket: 'This pair of objects ... is a unique survival from the seventeenth century. The portrait shows Margaret Laton, the wife of a yeoman of the King's Jewel House, about 1620. She is wearing the very same jacket.'[11] The portrait is thought to be by Marcus Gheeraerts the younger and the jacket is made of linen with fine embroidery and applied shiny spangles. The British Galleries were opened in 2001 and as part of the celebration there was a collaboration with the well-known UK-based textile company Sanderson (which has a royal warrant). It produced a promotional booklet, which stated on the back page:

> Elizabethan Collection – The
> V&A Elizabethan collection by
> Sanderson celebrates the shared
> design heritage and creative
> energy synonymous with two
> great names in British design.
> By choosing the very best
> Elizabethan design elements
> from the British Galleries of the
> Victoria & Albert Museum in
> London, Sanderson carries on
> a long tradition of craftsman-
> ship and commitment to quality.
> The focus of the collection is the
> Tudor and Stuart periods, famed
> for their love of rich colour, tex-
> ture and adornment.[12]

One fabric related to the pair of objects described above was a printed textile called Elizabeth based on the decorative motifs, including a pattern of swirling and coiling stems with acorns, strawberries, honeysuckle, pea pods, cornflowers, pansies and roses. There were accompanying furnishing fabrics, including Catherine, Boleyn, Seymour, Quadrille, Burleigh, Aragon, Hatton and Hardwick, made of a variety of materials including cotton, linen, hemp and silk. Associated wallpapers were also produced as part of the collection. The fabrics and wallpapers made full use of the British Galleries for inspiration, using all the characteristics of Elizabethan and Jacobean imagery and symbolism. Whilst mulberry trees were not directly referenced, one of the colourways of the fabric with the code PV8573/1CU did have a mulberry colour in its mix and was called Elizabeth Mulberry Olive Cut.

Numerous sources were viewed for this study in order to establish the use of mulberry imagery, and examples are rare. The V&A collections have a European example of a complex silk design with intertwined images of both mulberry leaves and fruits along with stylised peacock feathers. This piece of fabric was produced in 1904 and is from France and can be described as velvet brocade with silver gilt thread in the style of a Florentine fabric c.1500. A letter from the Commission séricicole internationale in France states that the manufacturing company Tassinari & Chatel is still in operation and has archives of the fabric at Chemin Roseaux, Fontaines Saint Martin.[13] In the same V&A collections there is an Elizabethan embroidered slip featuring what is undoubtedly the best example of a textile image featuring a mulberry (Illustration 10). This is not the original slip but an accurate reproduction of the image created by the charity Fine Cell Work, whose chairperson in 2009 was Lady Anne Tree. It is worked in wool on a canvas base and was made by a male prisoner as part of his rehabilitation. The actual slip – Museum Number MT.50-1972 – was on a canvas ground with silk and metal thread embroidery. The 'Material and Making' section of the V&A website states: 'Slips were small, usually floral motifs drawn onto canvas, then embroidered and cut out. They would be applied to a rich backing fabric such as velvet or satin.' This process is discussed and illustrated in Sian Evans's *To the Manor Reborn: The Transformation of Avebury Manor* in which a peacock feather coverlet was recreated by the Royal School of Needlework using Liberty's Hera fabric as inspiration.[14] Multiple slips were embroidered in wool crewel on a handwoven linen twill. In *Design and the Decorative Arts: Tudor and Stuart*

Britain, 1500–1714, bed coverlets are discussed and an illustration shows an example of quite graphic outlines of various plants, similar to the V&A mulberry slip.[15] It is labelled: 'A page of patterns for embroidery motifs 1632' and shows a page from *A Scholehouse for the Needle* by Richard Shorleyker. It suggests that the naturalistic motifs at first came via herbals.

By the seventeenth century, outline drawings and illustrations were being supplied by printers such as Peter Stent that could be used as guides or inspiration for embroidery. An early herbal entitled *The Herbal, or Generall Historie of Plantes* by John Gerard from 1597 contains plant images, as does 'the therd booke of Flower Fruits Beastes Birds and Flies exactly drawn', which is illustrated in *English Embroidery from The Metropolitan Museum of Art, 1580–1700: Twixt Art and Nature*.[16] This book gives a comprehensive account of embroidery in the Tudor and Jacobean periods and discusses furnishings and dress in the context of naturalistic representation. The publication was produced as part of an exhibition at the Bard Graduate Center for Studies in the Decorative Arts, Design and Culture which ran from December 2008 to April 2009. Some of the objects are illustrated and one such embroidery, entitled 'Adam and Eve in the Garden of Eden with Virtues' (pp. 268–269), might depict a mulberry tree (on the right of the three trees). The leaves on the tree do not look like vine leaves but are heart shaped and the fruits could be described as mulberry-like and are similar to those in the V&A mulberry slip. However, the annotation for the artefact states that the three trees are pomegranate (left), oak (middle) and grape (right). Given that the other two trees have been recorded reasonably correctly in terms of both fruit and leaf shapes, it would be more accurate to call the third tree a mulberry. Grapes are usually portrayed on vines, with the vine leaves depicted in black on white embroidered fabric called blackwork, which was apparently a favourite of Elizabeth I (see Burleigh in the Sanderson V&A collections). There are some examples in *English Embroidery from The Metropolitan Museum of Art* in which grapes have been accurately portrayed with vine leaves (which have a very specific shape). If these embroideries had been influenced by herbals it could be concluded that at the very least the leaf shape would have been recorded accurately. Mistakes like this example and the one at Knole (featured below in 'Zoffany and Soreau') do happen because such imagery is always open to interpretation and thus to debate.

7 English Mulberry blazer pocket with hand embroidered insignia

Sericulture, Hermès and the Golden Orb

Historic and contemporary images of silk production can be found throughout the world. The British Museum has a portfolio entitled *Vermis Sericus* (the silkworm) published by Phillip Galle (1537–1612) with illustrations by Jan van der Street (1523–1605) that visually maps the process of silk production in the sixteenth century. A reproduction image is available to purchase from Bridgeman Art Library entitled 'Women Lining Shelves with Mulberry Leaves for the Silkworms'. Further interesting sericulture images are available in facsimile reproduction including one called *A Bower of Mulberry Trees* (1854) by Hannah Cahoon (1781–1864) taken from an original Shaker spirit drawing housed at Hancock Shaker Village, Massachusetts, which featured in a 2012 auction.[17] In a more contemporary setting, the artist/illustrator Ann Bridges was awarded an Arts Council of Wales grant in 2006 to record, by illustration, the life cycle of the silkworm. This led to work for Cheshire County Council locating white mulberry trees for a proposed Year of the Garden project in 2008. She made numerous preparatory illustrations detailing the life of *Bombyx mori* from very small eggs to the silkworms and beyond. Ann Bridges' 'Spinning a Yarn – The Emperor's New Clothes Project' eventually created twenty beautiful framed drawings illustrating the life cycle from the egg to the thread, which travelled to small-scale venues in Wales at both Llandudno and Ruthin.[18] A sketch book with text annotations was also created and this detailed the location of some white mulberry leaf sources. One of particular note is the gardens at Bodelwyddan Castle, which have a mulberry lawn with both white and black mulberry trees (Bodelwyddan is not included in the Survey List). The interesting life cycle of *Bombyx mori* is obviously critical to the production of silk. The manufacturing processes and the complexity of the nurturing of silkworm eggs via metamorphosis to cocoons is detailed in a text by Silvio Farago.[19] The process now takes place on virtually an industrial scale with one hectare of mulberry tree plantation raising about 400,000 silkworms, which in turn produce 700 kilograms of fresh cocoons. After processing this creates about 100 kilograms of silk that can then be processed and woven into cloth. Silk is a highly desirable natural product and no part of the cocoon is wasted in the manufacturing process, waste fibre being used as insulation material in duvets that are retailed in Europe. The waste wood from the mulberry trees is made into composite material and manufactured into flooring (Illustration 11), which is marketed in the United Kingdom.

One of the most interesting and accurate depictions of mulberry leaves and their association with sericulture has been produced by Hermès – a beautifully embossed letter indicated two specific designs from the archives.[20] Hermès has a long association with silk scarves which have become iconic both for wearers and collectors. Scarf production began in 1928 and a fully illustrated history is documented in

8 English Mulberry tree located outside Mulberry headquarters, Somerset

Nadine Coleno's book, *The Hermès Scarf: History and Mystique.* Coleno writes:

> The Hermès scarf has considerable assets that help to preserve its balance and identity. The first of these is shape. Its French name, *carré*, means simply 'square'. The square is perfect, stable, simple and evenly proportioned, and lends itself to endless transformations – all qualities that have given it symbolic power since the dawn of time. The Japanese arts of origami and furoshiki (an ancient form of wrapping cloth) explore the hidden potential in this shape.[21]

The scarf is an ideal canvas for people to create images, and many famous artists and designers produced designs for the 1995 collections. One of these features intertwined mulberry leaves of both usual and biomorphic appearance, mulberry fruits and *Bombyx mori* in various developmental forms including silkworms and moths (but no cocoons). This is detailed in Illustration 12, which features a predominantly jade green colour with naturalistic looking images (a number of different colourways were available, including one with a lapis blue background and yellow leaves). Coleno continues:

> *L'Arbre de soie* ('Tree of Silk', Antoine de Jacquelot, 1995), *Au fil de la soie* ('Along the Silk Thread', Annie Faivre, 1995), *Soleil de soie* ('Silk Sun', Caty Latham-Audibert, 1995). All these designers pay homage to the legendary fabric that is silk. The Silk Road that ran from Asia to Europe was so named because silk was the most highly prized commodity carried by the merchants who travelled the route, trading it for ivory, horses and precious stones. It is said that silk was discovered around 3000 BC by a young Chinese empress who, when trying to remove a cocoon that had fallen into her cup of tea from a mulberry tree, found herself unwinding an endless and matchlessly fine thread.[22]

A relatively detailed account of silk production in various parts of the world is included in the book *Silk* by A. H. Gaddum.[23] This was produced under the auspices of a silk manufacturer located in Macclesfield, Cheshire, called H. T. Gaddum & Co. Interestingly, the antique dealer Thomas Coulborn & Sons had a rare nineteenth-century walnut silk cocoon specimen cabinet from France for sale in 2012, which had been in the ownership of the Gaddum family of Macclesfield.[24] Macclesfield has a significant heritage relating to silk, the town being an important manufacturer of silk goods in the eighteenth and nineteenth centuries, and it has a series of museums (including the Paradise Mill) which develop the story. An article in the *Macclesfield Express* detailed a quilt presented to Queen Victoria.[25] The coverlet was made of silk and had imagery on it to celebrate the Golden Jubilee with a substantial border depicting mulberry leaves, silk moths and mulberry fruits. In 1887, the *Macclesfield Courier* recorded the making of the item which was edged in gold with a defining text: 'Presented to her Most Gracious Majesty Queen Victoria, in the year of her jubilee MDCCCLXXXVII, by the women of Macclesfield, in the County of Cheshire'. The actual coverlet has been lost but the artwork for the original design was found among some discarded rubbish and kept for the Macclesfield museum's silk-related collection.

As mentioned in Chapter 1, in 2012 the V&A exhibited a cape made from the silk produced from the golden orb spider *Nephila madagascariensis*. In the accompanying book, *Golden Spider Silk*, Simon Peers writes:

> The cape is made with a variety of different embroidery stitches and fine appliqué effects. The thread used in weaving both textiles is first composed of 24 single threads drawn from 24 individual spiders. These threads are joined and twisted together in the 'silking' part of the process … The resulting work is the fruit of thousands of hours of collecting, 'silking', throwing and weaving the silk of millions of spiders.[26]

This is part of a truly amazing, intricate and time-consuming process which has resulted in an exceptional piece of craft. The imagery on the cape was detailed both in preparatory drawings and also photographs of the final detail. Like the Hermès silk square *L'Arbre de soie*, mentioned above, the cape has insect imagery which includes the spider responsible for making the silk, with flowing botanical forms – leaves and flowers symmetrically arranged around the central opening and tassels. The spiders are depicted with a thread coming from their spinnerets and this scroll work can be seen throughout the textile – the imagery tells a story in a visual language. The cape is stunningly bright yellow and reflects the colour of the perfectly symmetrical webs that the spiders produce in nature – there was no colour application in the making process nor were any colours applied in decoration. No one who sees the garment could fail to be impressed. Broadcaster and naturalist David Attenborough, even after everything he has seen on his world travels, was amazed and commented: 'Twenty-four female *Nephilas*, each sitting in her own little compartment, industriously spinning silk that is threaded through a tiny hole, wound on to bobbins and then woven, [have produced] what must surely be counted as one of the rarest and most glamorous of fabrics.'[27]

Zoffany and Soreau

Zoffany is a contemporary furnishings retailer which is in the same parent company as Sanderson and Morris & Co. It creates ranges in fabrics, wallpapers, paints, furniture, trimmings and carpets. In 2002, the company collaborated with the National Trust to produce a range of fabrics and wallpapers based on some of its most famous properties.[28] The first collection was launched and proved a success, with some of the profits going to the National Trust for the upkeep of their houses, gardens and services. The Zoffany designers took various interiors as inspiration from properties including Hardwick Hall, Felbrigg Hall, Oxburgh Hall and Knole. A collection of seven fabrics and associated wallpapers were designed using traditional motifs with sophisticated manufacturing, including state of the art weaving and finishing techniques. The project appeared to be the perfect collaboration between a fashionable and contemporary company and the tradition of the National Trust.

Some of the fabrics of note included Hardwick Hall Great Chamber, which was based on an Elizabethan slip fabric using botanical imagery (probably from herbals). The promotional literature states: 'The richly embroidered fabric features English flowers – roses, primroses, daffodils, cornflowers and acorns – on a textured background.' A further fabric from Hardwick was inspired by the Great Hall. The property that offered the greatest inspiration was Knole in Kent. Knole is famously associated with the Sackville West family and particularly Vita Sackville West. The house was built in the fifteenth century and was owned by Queen Elizabeth I, but she gifted the property in 1566

to her cousin, Thomas Sackville. Exceptional features of the house include the decorated stairwell and the plasterwork ceilings in various rooms including the Cartoon Gallery. The Gallery is described in the guidebook:

> The plasterwork ceiling by
> Richard Duggan differs from
> the others in having no square
> or intersecting panels, merely
> serpentine ribs which give a
> marvellous rippling effect of light
> and shade seen down the whole
> length of the Gallery. The spaces
> between the ribs are again filled
> by shallow reliefs of botanical
> emblems, probably taken by the
> plasterer from the woodcuts
> of some late sixteenth-century
> herbal.

It is almost certain that the images used at Knole of botanic material were sourced from both herbals and embroidery. It is of course very difficult precisely to source material directly to attach to plasterwork, although this has the potential for further study and is discussed in the context of Plas Mawr featured later in this chapter.

Four fabrics were created: Knole Spangle Bedroom, Knole King's Closet, Knole Drawing Room and finally Knole Cartoon Gallery. This last fabric was described by Zoffany thus:

> Both the woven textile and elegant wallpaper were taken from
> the famous plasterwork ceiling
> of the Cartoon Gallery at Knole.
> The interpretation features a
> trellis framework entwined with
> mulberries, leaves and bold flowers in sculptural effect. The fabric
> is available in three colour ways,
> and the wallpaper is available in
> five colour ways. (Illustrations 13
> and 14)

A further fabric called Linen Press was apparently inspired by Hardwick Hall and completes the fabric range – the wall coverings also include Felbrigg and Oxburgh papers. In the Knole fabric and wallpaper the graphic mulberry imagery is very convincing and the fruits are the correct scale; even the leaves have a shape that could be considered mulberry-like. However, when you view the plasterwork ceiling at Knole and look at more detailed photographs it becomes apparent that the imagery on the ceiling is probably not of mulberry fruit but rather bunches of grapes. This was confirmed by a letter from Dr Claire Gapper, a plasterwork

9 English fabric from Fired Earth, called 'Mulberry Trees'

ceiling expert, who indicated that the plants are more likely to be grapes or even hops because of the presence of tendrils.[29] These are found on vines and climbers but are never found on mulberry trees (neither *Morus nigra* nor *Morus alba*). It would appear that the designers at Zoffany produced the design with creativity rather than accurate representation.

A second series of designs was launched by Zoffany in 2005 using four further National Trust houses: Ham House, Erddig, Packwood House and Nostell Priory. Zoffany describes the collection as 'five weaves and seven wallpapers sourced from original National Trust references ... including richly textured damasks, velvets and appliqué silks and also lavish wallpapers that resemble iridescent silk, wood grain and architectural trompe l'œil.'[30] One such paper inspired by Nostell Priory was detailed in the promotional text as adapted from one

of the 'India Papers' – a hand-painted Chinese paper imported to the West by the East India Company and used in one of the bedrooms of Nostell Priory when they were redecorated by Thomas Chippendale in the late eighteenth century. This is illustrated in Dawn Jacobson's book *Chinoiserie*, with further text detailing Mr and Mrs David Garrick and their commission of Chippendale furniture based on East India Company chintzes which they had received as a gift (David Garrick is featured in greater detail in Chapter 5, below).[31] The paper called Nostell Priory depicted a flowering tree and is available in six colourways in a wide width (69 cm wide). One such wallpaper with a yellow ground and pink flowers has the code NTP06005 and is extremely authentic in appearance. The India papers are interesting because quite often they feature sericulture practice in that they portray images from the daily life of those who painted the scenes – mainly Chinese artists and artisans. There is a good example in Felbrigg Hall, which has a Chinese bedroom with hand-painted wallpaper from China, and circumstantially also has a mulberry tree (Survey List 96). There is also sumptuous wallpaper in a bedroom at Harewood House (not featured in the Survey List), which clearly shows Chinese figures in the process of harvesting mulberry leaves for silk production. Clearly it was the fashion of the day to have these papers imported by the East India Company. In fact, Sir Francis Sykes of Basildon Park (Survey List 55) made a considerable amount of money trading goods for the East India Company, and Chinese ceramics and aesthetics became the vogue, with Thomas Chippendale stating in 1754 that Chinese was one of three current design styles. Both the East and West India companies traded in commodities including tea, sugar, spices and ceramics – the papers being a lucrative sideline. The Harewood House bedroom is featured in an article in *World of Interiors*, which states:

> Harewood House's 'Indian paper' was in fact made in the region of Canton and depicts scenes of Chinese rural life – contented peasants manufacture porcelain and silk, grow tea and, as seen here, harvest rice. The paper's colours have survived intact for more than two centuries on account of the mineral pigments used in the paints, notably malachite and azurite.[32]

Malachite was used for a green pigment and azurite (like lapis) used for a blue. These wallpapers are also featured in an interesting National Trust restoration project at Avebury Manor. There was an accompanying television series produced by the BBC with Penelope Keith and Paul Martin, alongside Russell Sage (interior designer) and 'experts' Dan Cruickshank and Anna Whitelock. The hand-painted wallpaper was used to transform the dining room in the Georgian manner using modern papers produced in a similar way as the originals at Wuxi, China. The National Trust book states:

> Individual panels were made up of smaller hand-made sheets of paper, traditionally made from mulberry bark and bamboo, then treated with an application of fish glue to control the take up of paint. The background colour is painted first, the landscape, water and mountains in loose shading, leaving spaces for the figures, buildings and trees.[33]

The restoration team also used a reference paper that is housed in the Peabody Essex Museum at Salem, Massachusetts, which was originally located at Avebury. These narrative papers were sometimes produced to order and gifted – apparently George, 1st Earl Macartney, who was the first British ambassador to Beijing, gave papers to Thomas Coutts around 1794, and this paper is still in place on the walls of the Coutts bank boardroom in London (it also features images of silk production). In turn, these images from the India papers were transferred to furniture, including side cabinets produced around 1820 with views of mulberry-leaf harvesting painted on the doors. These very occasionally come on to the antiques market – for example, Partridge Fine Arts had a japanned cabinet for sale in 1989.

Isaak Soreau (1604–1644?) was an artist who worked in the still life genre, alongside other artists in Europe including Jacob van Hulsdonck and Sebastien Stoskopff. Soreau has been selected here because there is evidence that there may be images of mulberries in his painting. He used fruit extensively in his work and lived during the Jacobean period, although not in the United Kingdom. Soreau is well known for his horizontal presentation of fruit, flowers and objects (blue and white ceramics, baskets, glass and pewter) in detailed realistic studies and spatial arrangements. His pictures are very formulaic, having repeat components rearranged and altered from painting to painting. They are also relatively rare, with fewer than thirty being identified, and not a great deal is known about

10 English wool embroidery of mulberry tree, by Fine Cell Work

his life, although it is recorded that he was the son of Daniel Soreau who was a merchant, architect and painter. Daniel left Antwerp and lived in both Frankfurt and Hanua (1599), so this is probably where Isaak and his brother were born. The exact date of his death is not accurately known but because he produced so little it is assumed that he died young.[34] Many of his paintings are not dated and the only signed example is in the Schlossmuseum collection in Schwerin, Germany, and is dated 1638. Some of his identified pictures are located in established galleries and museums – in Europe these include the Ashmolean Museum, Oxford; Musée du Petit Palais, Paris; and Hamburg Art Museum. In the USA there are also panels at the Virginia Museum of Fine Art; Cincinnati Museum of Art; Walters Art Museum, Baltimore; the Museum of Fine Arts, Boston; and the Norton Simon Museum, Pasadena. In addition, a significant number of his works are in private collections and can be tracked via Artnet.com,[35] which gives details of sale locations (often in large auction houses such as Sotheby's or Christie's) and annotated illustrations of the paintings. Two of the most promising works in terms of potential mulberries came into the temporary ownership of the dealers John Mitchell of London, located in Old Bond Street. The first is a painting – oil on panel – which shows a glass vase with flowers including tulips, a basket of various grapes and, interestingly, a small blue and white tea bowl (a Wanli bowl) filled with fruit that look remarkably like mulberries.[36] In fact, the review of the National Gallery exhibition *Art in Seventeenth Century Holland* in the *Burlington Magazine* features this picture and specifically mentions mulberries.[37] This painting was sold by the dealers in 1990. The second picture, in an ebony frame – oil on uncradled panel – is called *A Still Life of Apricots and Plums with a Vase of Tulips and a Wild Rose on a Bench*. It shows on the wooden bench an image of a leaf with some berries, which have yet to be completely identified but look like blackberries. Sometimes it is almost impossible to be completely sure, but certainly mulberry trees were grown at the time and the fruit was highly regarded and would have been available. In certain pictures it can be identified with reasonable assurance. The symbolic meanings of the fruit and flowers in Soreau's work have been analysed – particularly the notion of the transient nature of material wealth when viewed alongside the ephemeral character of nature.

Isaak Soreau's berries have been identified as various soft fruit including raspberries, blackberries, mulberries and wild strawberries. Raspberries have been identified in the Oxford and Hamburg examples, being described as such by Fred Meijer in *Dutch and Flemish Still-Life Paintings*.[38] Blackberries (which can be confused with mulberries) have been identified in a picture sold at Christie's New York on 14 January 1993, and mulberries have been identified in a Soreau picture at the Walters Art Museum, Baltimore. Finally, wild strawberries feature in a picture at Christie's sale on 16 December 1998, which was described as 'bunches of grapes and vine leaves on a pewter platter, parrot tulips in a glass, wild strawberries in a Wanli Kraak porcelain bowl, plums, cherries, a fly, a butterfly and a dragonfly on a wooden ledge'. In many cases in Soreau's work it would have been impossible to paint all the natural components at any one time because of seasonality – his pictures are generally composites. In many studies the particular type of berry does not appear in the title – for example, the Virginia Museum of Art painting is entitled *Still Life with Grapes, Flowers, and Berries in a Wanli Bowl* (*c*.1620), while the painting at the Ashmolean Museum is simply *Still Life of Fruit and Flowers*. The painting at Schwerin Staatliches Museum is called *Still Life with Grapes and Porcelain Bowl*.

11 Oriental mulberry wood composite flooring sample

A significant number of Soreau's paintings repeat particular items. The Wanli tea bowl appears in a significant number of his oil on wood panels. Sometimes the small bowl appears with a larger blue-and-white bowl as is the case in the Ashmolean panel. It is more common to find the small tea bowl on its own filled with various berries and decorative leaves. Like so many objects portrayed in paintings these objects have an attached history which can become a study in its own right – as was the case with the *Making and Meaning* exhibition organised around Holbein's *Ambassadors*, which was held at the National Gallery, London in 1997–1998.[39] The notes attached to the Isaak Soreau entry in the Virginia Museum of Fine Arts catalogue state:

> Soreau's blue-and-white bowl
> represents porcelain that was
> exported from China to Europe at
> the time; in fact, the bowl bears
> the name Wanli, the emperor
> of China from 1572 to 1619.
> Dutch artists making fashion-
> able Delftware adapted Chinese
> patterns, among them Soreau's
> long-legged white deer sur-
> rounded by blue foliage.[40]

In fact, this practice continues with the Dutch company Tichelaar Makkum, which is still manufacturing in Holland (Illustration 15) and makes near-identical tea bowls to the one featured in the Soreau paintings. Kraak porcelain is a type of Chinese ware produced in the Wanli period that was intended for European markets. The exact origins of the word Kraak are uncertain, but it is known that it was generally not used in the inventories of the Dutch East India Company. It could have been a name that was associated with Portuguese ships or even the Irish ships called currachs. The porcelain was made in Jingdezhen and varied in quality from the mass-produced (Illustration 16) to special orders. The process of ceramic manufacture in this specialist centre was featured in *To the Manor Reborn: The Transformation of Avebury Manor* when the team ordered a special armorial tea service for Avebury.[41] It states in the accompanying book:

> Chinese porcelain was first devel-
> oped over 1000 years ago and
> was greatly valued for its hard-
> ness, translucency and delicacy
> of colour. The city of Jingdezhen,
> considered the birthplace of
> this type of porcelain, has one
> million inhabitants, of whom

> 300,000 are involved in porcelain
> production, many of them using
> traditional techniques and skills.

The characteristic of classic Kraakware is decorative panels in blue and white featuring flowers and animals that flow around the body of the piece. Very often the base has chatter marks which result from the finishing turning tool hitting the leather-hard ceramic when the base is being footed. There are significant similarities between the ware produced for the European market and that sent to Japan from China, a number of old Japanese tea ceremony bowls being the same as examples of Kraakware in Dutch museums. As mentioned above, the Dutch company Tichelaar Makkum makes both blue monochrome and polychrome reproductions of Kraakware. The company is famous for being one of the oldest established in the world, having been in continuous production since 1594. It is still successful today, producing both classic and contemporary products for international markets. Its entire history and archival material has been produced in Dutch (with English summaries) in a tour de force publication (two volumes, boxed) by Pieter Jan Tichelaar. The history is fully illustrated and shows the development of majolica wares from the early period to the present day.[42] A contemporary artist called Trisha Hardwick works in the Soreau genre, painting (usually in oils on linen panel) fruit including mulberries (Illustration 17 and front cover), strawberries, raspberries and cherries in various oriental bowls, including Kraakware.[43]

Plasterwork – Motto and Blackbird

Certain properties featured in the survey were targeted for additional information regarding their ceilings and the motifs found within the work. The properties which had both mulberry trees and the most interesting ceilings included Chastleton House (Survey List 8) and Westwood Manor (Survey List 16). Chastleton House was, and to a certain extent still is, a hidden gem in the National Trust's portfolio of properties.[44] Being located in the Cotswolds and having a walled garden it is an ideal site for a mulberry tree. The house is Jacobean and has a range of plasterwork ceilings of different sizes and complexity. Perhaps the most interesting is to be found in the Long Gallery, which has a spectacular barrel-vaulted ceiling. It states in the guidebook:

> The ceiling is constructed from
> a conventional armature of ribs
> and split laths, to which a coarse

12 French silk scarf from Hermès, called 'L'Arbre de Soie'

overmantel and ceiling with multiple surfaces that feature fruit imagery including pears, figs, grapes and some mulberry-like fruit similar to those found in the Plas Mawr image discussed below.

Other properties also have interesting material but for different reasons, including the property at Tyntesfield (Survey List 92), which has examples of fruit-based imagery in the library/study. There are also some impressive naturalistic botanic carvings in a frieze in Mrs Gibbs's Room, made from boxwood and illustrated in the Tyntesfield guidebook produced by the National Trust.[45] The property at Tissington (Survey List 60) has a woodland-inspired plasterwork frieze created by George Bankart (1866–1929) for the architect Arnold Bidlake Mitchell (1863–1944) in the library – this is illustrated in the Tissington Hall guidebook[46] and it also featured in an article in *House & Garden*.[47] George Bankart was part of the Arts and Crafts movement alongside Ernest Gimson (1864–1919), who was also interested in plasterwork (he used it on his furniture in the form of gesso), and he is known to have visited various historic houses with decorative ceilings, including Speke Hall, Haddon Hall, Hardwick, Knole and Chastleton.

The house at Loseley Park, Guildford, was thought to have been built to entertain Elizabeth I. Much of the house remains intact and is still the family home of the More-Molyneux family. The family history starts in essence with Sir Christopher More whose son Sir William More (1520–1600) built the property. The family tree features in the Loseley Park guidebook.[48] The house is open to the public and has survived into the twenty-first century mainly due to the estate becoming a well-run business concentrating on farming and dairy products. The house has a collection of significant rooms, furniture and paintings. Of particular interest are the individual portraits of James I and Anne of Denmark by John de Critz (1552–1642), which are housed in the Great Hall. Two fire surrounds are noteworthy. The first in the Great Hall, whilst not being spectacular, does have a significant panel with relevance to this study. The Loseley Park guidebook states:

base of lime, hair and sand was applied. The pattern of ribs seems then to have been pressed from the mould into the second coat of plaster. One mould was rotated to create each 'repeat' of the pattern, and the marks left by the edges of the mould can be seen in many places.

A cast section was entered into the collections of the V&A and a similar pattern exists at the gatehouse at Oriel College, Oxford. Certain sections of the ceiling, particularly around the windows, have a twisting stalk of various botanics, including pea pods, figs, pears, apples, apricots and possibly some mulberries (although they could equally be hops or grapes). Nearly the same imagery is on the ceilings at Westwood Manor – a smaller-scale manor house with ceilings that are more extravagant than you would expect for its stature. The King's Room has a magnificent

> The motto *Morus tarde moriens morum cito moriturum* around the mulberry tree is, of course, a pun on the family name More and means 'The mulberry tree dying slowly, the fruit about to die quickly.' The family, like the tree, will survive for a long time,

but the individual Mores, like
the fruit, enjoy a relatively brief
existence.[49]

The plasterwork is shown in Illustration 18. In addition to this mulberry image and motto there is further evidence of mulberries in the Drawing Room, a picture of which is shown in the guidebook. It contains a magnificent plasterwork ceiling with elaborate frieze. This frieze contains various family emblems including moorhens, cockatrice and mulberry trees. The second important fireplace in the Drawing Room is elaborate and features coloured crests, and is after a design by Holbein the Younger (1497–1543); being carved out of chalk it is a magnificent example of three-dimensional sculptural work. Holbein's design has been considered as inspiration for embroiderers and is cited in Morrall and Watt's *English Embroidery from the Metropolitan Museum of Art, 1580–1700*, where it states that his decorative scrollwork started to appear in blackwork in the 1540s.[50] In Loseley Park, on either side of the fire surround, there is a pair of Maid of Honour chairs, the cushions of which are believed to have been embroidered by Elizabeth I. Other significant embroideries include a bed cover of the William and Mary period, which has a remarkable

similarity with those of the Chelsea Textiles company, a contemporary company specialising in needlework sometimes using antique embroidery as inspiration, such as their Pomegranate and Blue Flower pillow.

Alongside these pictorial images of mulberries there are also various black mulberry trees in the garden of Loseley Park (Survey List 20). One tree was thought to have been planted by Elizabeth I on one of her four visits, and apparently nearly died during the Second World War, but it still survives. The mulberry tree is symbolic for the family and the trees have become associated with the More-Molyneux line at Loseley Park. As a matter of family concern, a further six trees have been planted for insurance purposes.[51] A tree planted in 1932 by Queen Mary succumbed to the hurricane of 1987.[52] This event had a considerable impact on a significant number of trees in the United Kingdom and many mulberry trees did not survive it. This is discussed further in the next chapter.

A further mulberry tree image (tentatively identified) exists at Plas Mawr. This property, protected by Cadw, the Welsh Government's historic environment service, is a medieval masterpiece, a town house within the walls of Conwy. Detailed plans of the house, with

15 Dutch Tichelaar
Makkum bowl with
mulberry fruit and leaves

16 Chinese Ming porcelain
bowl from the Wanli
period

17 English painting,
Mulberries and Cream
(2013), by Trisha
Hardwick
By permission of Trisha
Hardwick

cutaway views, are presented on the inside cover of the Plas Mawr guidebook, which proclaims the building to be the finest Elizabethan town house in the British Isles.[53] The residence is associated with Robert Wynn (1520–1598) and is famous for the quality and the quantity of plasterwork within the building, the earliest date recorded in the plasterwork (on an overmantel) being 1577. The plasterwork is extraordinary and includes multiple images featuring heraldic emblems comprising animals such as an eagle, boar and stag's head. There are also botanical images including the Tudor rose and leaf shapes. The form of a bird with a plant combines the two elements, and this one is possibly a mulberry. The plant looks very much like the tree featured in the mulberry slip found in the collections of the V&A (Illustration 10). Secondly, the image is associated with a bird, and it is well known that mulberry fruit is irresistible to birds, particularly the blackbird (*Turdus merula*) – they sing with apparent joy when they are collecting the fruit.[54] Finally, there is a beautiful late fifteenth-century misericord wood carving at Ripon Cathedral that features birds pecking on mulberry fruit.

Conclusion

The range of objects featuring mulberry imagery considered in this chapter has obviously changed over time in terms of both the actual artefact but also the intent behind the making and crafting of the artefact. The earliest work is evident on both soft (textile) and

18 English plasterwork
from Loseley Park,
Guildford, Surrey

hard (plasterwork) surfaces and has in essence a decorative function within the context of a relatively wealthy Elizabethan home. The coloured embroidered slip in the collections of the V&A is a small item which has been created by hand with care and attention to detail. It is a sampler that was intended to be applied to a larger piece of functional fabric. A decorative bed cover both keeps the user warm and also has meaning in terms of the connection with the maker and the potential for aesthetic delight on the part of the viewer. Bed covers can have a symbolic meaning and can often tell a story, as has been discussed by Grayson Perry with regard to the quilt.[55] A bed cover in the collections of the Kentucky Historical Society is called the Graveyard Quilt, and is by Elizabeth Roseberry Mitchell. It is chequerboard in construction with a graveyard surrounded by a picket fence located in

19 English wool scarf
showing Mulberry
logotype

the middle. Family members are depicted as appliqué coffin shapes along the outer edge of the quilt. As they passed away their coffin was unpicked and stitched into the graveyard – the 'ghosts' of the dead people being evident along the outside edge. The story attached to the object clearly adds resonance to its content and meaning.

The interior world in the Elizabethan and Jacobean period would have been relatively dark and decorative elements in interiors obviously had greater impact because they provided visual stimulation – the flickering candle flame would pick up silver thread in a textile. The image on the mulberry slip and the decorative piece at Plas Mawr have certain similarities, both being out of scale and naive in form. They have a characteristically Elizabethan look due to the initial drawing and flattened perspective. In other images of the period, accuracy of portrayal was important and this can be seen in Soreau's representation of mulberries in the Wanli bowl. Still life painters of the period were required to create images that could be read by the owners of the picture – they are like representational photographs. These are the images most like those found in scientific studies or botanical illustration and featured in Chapter 5, below. Many of the images discussed in this chapter have changed over time because they are decorative rather than scientific: the purpose of the object dictates the decoration or depiction alongside the design and style of the period. Some objects created in celebration of an event, such as the Macclesfield coverlet for Queen Victoria, are representative of the taste and fashion of the time and clearly the work can be placed in the Victorian age, being elaborate and quite heavily decorated.

As we move further towards the twenty-first century the images become more abstract and influenced by various contemporaneous art movements. For example, the Hermès scarf, whilst being an accurate representation of the silkworm's life cycle, is represented in a Warholian manner using odd and unusual colourways. The work becomes slightly more abstracted and difficult to read. The most contemporary use of the mulberry tree is also the most simple – the Mulberry Company logotype (Illustration 19). It would be hard to recognise anything other than a tree in this image, which is quite childlike. The pictogram of the tree is an image that can be recognised and read throughout the world. Recently the company's tree logotype has been refined by the Construct design company, and this has been carried through in all the company styling, featuring the legend 'EST. 1971'.[56] The tree logotype transcends language barriers and is instantly recognisable – it is part of the brand identity reflecting both a style and a lifestyle. The company has a living logo outside its headquarters in the form of a black mulberry tree which validates the company name. A similar mulberry tree image appears on a plaque at 28 High Street, Woodstock, in the Cotswolds. This signifies the property's position in a historic walk and it has a very old mulberry tree in the garden.[57]

A factor which changes over time is clearly the way objects are manufactured. The decorative work detailed in this chapter produced by Fired Earth, Sanderson, Chelsea Textiles and Zoffany is influenced by the first Elizabethan period while being manufactured in the second. These objects are made with sophisticated machinery that ironically makes the items look handmade. This involves weaving, machine embroidery and printing, as seen in the Zoffany wallpaper, which looks handblocked in a William Morris tradition but is mass manufactured. Social and economic factors have clearly influenced the objects and often this narrative needs fuller explanation. A good example of this is the Loseley Park overmantel, which has real significance for the More-Molyneux family because of their history and its connection with living mulberry trees. Material culture suggests that most objects with any content are time-sensitive. Most of the objects featured in this study can be dated without any contextual detail – they are reflective of their period and the people who used them. It is entirely predictable that mulberry trees should find their way into the decorative arts because nature and the naturalistic have always been sources of inspiration for makers, designers and artists. Images of mulberry trees and their associated products have moved from relatively small audiences to mass markets. Finally, it is only when we recognise the detail attached to crafted objects that the craft and skill involved in making them can be assessed. No better example exists than the yellow spider silk cape which is a remarkable and beautiful textile created with skill and endurance – an object out of its time in terms of quality, and unique in the truest sense.

Notes to Chapter 2

1   Thomas A. Graves (ed.), *Seeing Things Differently: An Exhibition Catalogue* (Little Compton, RI: Winterthur Publications and Fort Church Publishers, 1992). The 'Change over Time' section is from pp. 22–31 (p. 22).
2   www.mulberry.com (accessed 1 September 2012).
3   Private correspondence dated 29 January 2009 to the author from Roger Saul (Sharpham Park).
4   Saul, *Mulberry at Home*, p. 6.
5   Louisa Peacock, 'Mulberry: From Somerset to Singapore', *Daily Telegraph*, 9 December 2010, www.telegraph.co.uk/finance/newsbysector/retailandconsumer/8191192/Mulberry-from-Somerset-to-Singapore.html (accessed 19 September 2012).
6   Georgia Fendley (ed.), *Mulberry: Est. 1971* (Bath: Mulberry Company (Design) Limited, 2011). The tree is shown on p. 197 and the factory is featured on pp. 198–227.
7   Chelsea Flower Show catalogue, 24–27 May 1994. In the archive of the Royal Horticultural Society.
8   'Rear View', with a photograph by Simon Norfolk, *Weekend Telegraph*, 24 May 1994, p. 44.
9   'Mulberry Moves On', *Daily Telegraph*, 9 June 1994, p. 18.
10 Michael Parry, *Morris & Co.: A Revolution in Decoration* (Denham: Morris & Co., 2011). See 'An Enduring Brand Image' (p. 60).
11 Dinah Winch, *The British Galleries, 1500–1900: A Guide Book* (London: V&A Publications, 2001). See the section 'Dressing for Magnificence, 1600–1630' (p. 20).
12 Sanderson promotional brochure (2001) for the Elizabethan Collection, in collaboration with the V&A.
13 Private correspondence dated 25 February 2008 to the author from Dr Gerard Chavancy.
14 Sian Evans, *To the Manor Reborn: The Transformation of Avebury Manor* (London: National Trust Books, 2011). The photograph is on p. 93.
15 Snodin and Styles, *Design and the Decorative Arts: Tudor and Stuart Britain, 1500–1714*. See illustration on p. 138.
16 Andrew Morrall and Melinda Watt (eds), *English Embroidery from the Metropolitan Museum of Art, 1580–1700: Twixt Art and Nature. An Exhibition Catalogue* (New York: Bard Graduate Center for Studies in the Decorative Arts, Design and Culture, 2008). See illustration on p. 213.
17 Auction Catalogue: The McCue Shaker Collection, Willis Henry Auctions, 8 September 2012. Held at Hancock Shaker Village, Pittsfield, Massachusetts. Lot 38 is featured on p. 27 and achieved a price of $2,200.
18 'Spinning a Yarn' and other associated illustrations were generously provided by Ann Bridges for reference (correspondence dated 13 March 2008). See www.annbridges.com (accessed 2 September 2012).
19 Schoeser, *Silk*, 'Sericulture' (Silvio Farago) and 'Silk in History' (pp. 60–65).
20 Private correspondence from Hermès, Paris, dated 11 April 2008 to the author from Isabelle Guillot.
21 Nadine Coleno, *The Hermès Scarf: History and Mystique* (London: Thames & Hudson, 2009), pp. 22–23.
22 Ibid., p. 190.

23 A. H. Gaddum, *Silk: How and Where it is Produced* (Macclesfield: H. T. Gaddum & Company, 1989) (booklet).

24 Thomas Coulborn & Sons Ltd is based at Vesey Manor, Sutton Coldfield, in the West Midlands and has a website featuring details of the antiques for sale, with a brief history. See www.coulborn.com. Details of the specimen cabinet (accessed 12 October 2012) are no longer available.

25 Olive Ambrose, 'Quilt Revives Memories of Victoria', in 'Silk Threads', *Macclesfield Express*, 4 July 2007, p. 40. 'Silk Threads' is a weekly column by Macclesfield Silk Museums.

26 Simon Peers, *Golden Spider Silk* (London: V&A Publications, 2012), pp. 44–45.

27 Ibid. The David Attenborough quotation is taken from the Foreword.

28 Brochure produced by Zoffany in collaboration with the National Trust entitled *The National Trust Collection* (2002), with styling by Harriet Moissett. The colour promotional booklet was produced for the launch of the collection and includes all the fabrics and wallpapers in the range plus some contextual material regarding the houses.

29 Private correspondence dated 18 August 2009 to the author from Dr Claire Gapper.

30 Taken from a press release in 2005 produced by Zoffany in collaboration with the National Trust.

31 Dawn Jacobson, *Chinoiserie* (London: Phaidon Press, 1993). The Nostell Priory bedroom is featured in a full-page illustration on p. 140 and dated 1769.

32 Matthew Dennison, 'Paper Trail', *World of Interiors*, 28.7 (2008), pp. 68–77 (p. 68).

33 Evans, *To the Manor Reborn*, p. 156.

34 *Gallery Notes* (Spring 2008). Produced and published by John Mitchell Fine Paintings, London.

35 Artnet.com. There is a charge for using their 'Market Alerts'.

36 The painting as featured in the *Gallery Notes* (n. 34, above) is nearly identical to a picture in Walters Art Museum, Baltimore (thewalters.org). Both pictures have what appear to be mulberry fruits in a blue and white Wanli bowl.

37 'Current and Forthcoming Exhibitions', *Burlington Magazine*, 118.884 (1976), pp. 785–787.

38 Fred G. Meijer, *Dutch and Flemish Still-Life Paintings* (Amsterdam: Waanders Publishers, in collaboration with the Ashmolean Museum, Oxford, 2003), p. 281.

39 Susan Foister, Ashok Roy and Martin Wyld, *Making and Meaning: Holbein's Ambassadors, An Exhibition Catalogue* (London: National Gallery Publications, 1997).

40 Selections from Anne B. Barriault and Kay M. Davidson, *The Virginia Museum of Fine Arts* (Charlottesville, Va.: University of Virginia Press, 2007), pp. 212–213.

41 Evans, *To the Manor Reborn*, p. 158.

42 Pieter Jan Tichelaar, *Fries Aardewerk Tichelaar Makkum*, 2 vols (Leiden: Primavera Press, 2004). Examples of early Kraakware reproductions are shown in the various plates from p. 95, including no. 1028 (29) in the volume for developments from 1868 to 1963.

43 Trisha Hardwick has had solo exhibitions of her work at the Wren Gallery, Burford, Oxfordshire (2012) and the Contemporary Fine Art Gallery, Eton, Berkshire (2013). Her work features exquisitely painted fruit including raspberries, strawberries, cherries, figs, quince and mulberries, amongst other fruit varieties. Full details can be seen on her website, www.trisha-hardwick.com (accessed 27 September 2013).

44 Chastleton features in a *Country Life* article that also highlights a mulberry tree: 'An ancient-looking black mulberry lies along the ground, deceiving us, as they often do: mulberries in Britain are very prone to leaning over, looking old before their time.' See Steven Desmond, 'On a Cold and Frosty Morning', with photographs by Allan Pollok-Morris, *Country Life*, 12–19 December 2012, pp. 88–93 (p. 93).

45 Francis Greenacre and Stephen Ponder, *Tyntesfield Guidebook* (London: National Trust, 2005). The illustration is on p. 25.

46 Richard FitzHerbert, *Tissington Hall Guidebook* (Derby: Derbyshire Countryside Ltd, 2003), illustration on p. 17 (full page) with detail on p. 18.

47 Roger White, 'Tissington Hall, Derbyshire', *House & Garden*, August 2012, p. 69.

48 The More-Molyneux family, *Loseley Park Guidebook* (Derby: Heritage House Group Ltd, 1994). The family tree is on p. 15.

49 Ibid, p. 8.

50 Morrall and Watt (eds), *English Embroidery from the Metropolitan Museum of Art, 1580–1700*, p. 44.

51 Private correspondence dated 3 August 2006 to the author from Michael More-Molyneux.

52 Private correspondence dated 21 July 2005 to the author from Michael More-Molyneux.

53 Diane M. Williams (series editor), *Plas Mawr, Conwy Guidebook* (Cardiff: Cadw, Welsh Assembly Government, 2008).

54 Geoff Sample, *Garden Bird Songs and Calls* (London: HarperCollins Publishers, 2000).

55 Jeremy Webster and Grayson Perry, *The Charms of Lincolnshire*, exhibition catalogue, produced in collaboration with The Collection, Lincoln (Lincoln: Lincolnshire County Council and the Arts Council of Great Britain, 2006). The quilt is illustrated on p. 8.

56 www.creative-inspiration.co.uk, 'Recent Projects Special'. The article, which illustrated letterheaded paper, packaging, bag clasps, the 40th anniversary book and a shop front with new, refined (very subtle) modifications (accessed 15 October 2010), is no longer available.

57 See Tom Jennings, 'Take Tour of Town's Historic Buildings', 21 January 2012, which has details of the plaques (designed by Giles MacDonald in Portland Stone) placed around Woodstock for its historic walk. It says of Cromwell's House, No. 28 High Street: 'Oliver Cromwell is said to have stayed in the house during the Civil War and William III was entertained in the house in 1698. From 1675, it was occupied by John Cary, a lawyer and agent for aristocrats, who claimed to have been a royal servant for every 17th century king'. The plaque (no. 7 in the trail) has a carved low relief mulberry tree: 'The mulberry tree design refers to an Act of Parliament, which said homes could have alcohol sold from them if a mulberry tree was planted in the garden': www.oxfordmail.co.uk/archive/2012/01/21/9485152. Take_tour_of_town_s_historic_buildings/ (accessed 23 May 2015). See also, 'Historic Trail: Woodstock' (2012), a leaflet produced by West Oxfordshire District Council and Woodstock Town Council.

20 English mulberry wood
cross section slice

Technique and Maker

Introduction

Mulberry wood is a well-behaved timber though it can be prone to splitting if not treated correctly (Illustration 20). Some contemporary furniture designers/makers have indicated that the wood is amenable and ages well. For example, John Makepeace has written that when he has used mulberry wood it was both easy to work and took a good finish. He has used it on a number of occasions mainly for table tops. Very occasionally there are examples of mulberry wood in older pieces of furniture – for example, a beautiful piece made by Gordon Russell (1892–1980) in his workshop at Broadway in the Cotswolds in 1927. Details of his life and work are featured in Maureen Butler's *Gordon Russell: Vision and Reality*, and two similar cabinets are illustrated on pages 18 and 19.[1] The cabinet with mulberry still exists and is in the collections of the V&A (Museum Number 428-1965, which is in storage at Olympia). Working drawings describe the cabinet as follows:

> Design for a writing cabinet,
> made in walnut, with panels of
> burr elm, and mulberry borders.
> Front elevation, side elevation,
> detail of interior, scale 3 inches to
> 1 foot. Full scale details of mould-
> ings, hinge arrangements, drawer
> fronts, legs and stretchers.

The piece was stamped, dispatched and numbered 651 and the pen-and-ink drawings are also in the collections of the V&A (Museum Number E.322-1977). The piece is recorded in the Gordon Russell Museum archive.[2] Photographs provided by the museum indicate that it is similar to the Paris Exhibition cabinet designed in 1924 which was awarded a gold medal, the cabinet being made out of traditional English hardwoods such as walnut, box, yew and laburnum oysters. The mulberry in the 1927 cabinet is in blocks of solid wood used to frame the burr elm panels and has stained oak bosses at each corner. The attention to detail is remarkable. Handmade hinges are used throughout, with silver drop handles (Birmingham 1927 hallmarks) and a hinge on the front stamped LYGON (after the Lygon Arms, Broadway). Russell's work of this period is quintessentially English and it seems entirely appropriate that mulberry should be part of the furniture's construction and composition. During his long life Russell delivered a series of addresses concerning skill, design, honesty and the crafts. All these topics are of relevance to this chapter.

The furniture historian Adam Bowett has stated that furniture recorded as mulberry is extremely rare in the seventeenth century, with only one small late-seventeenth-century table being identified. He indicates that, generally, mulberry was not of interest to furniture makers because the wood was usually quite small in size and therefore seldom used.[3] He

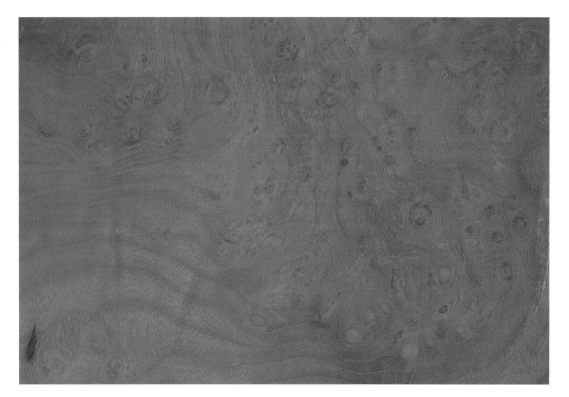

writes in his book *English Furniture, 1660–1714 from Charles II to Queen Anne* that mulberry is:

> A nonsense term used in the antiques trade to describe maple, elm or ash veneers which have been stained with nitric acid and lampblack to produce a spectacular mottled or 'tortoiseshell' effect. There is no historical evidence for the use of mulberry in fine cabinet-making, although there is no reason why it could not be used for treen or novelty items.[4]

He goes on to refer to another member of the mulberry family, Fustic (*Chlorophora tinctoria*), which is sometimes called dyers mulberry because of its yellow stain. The rarity of mulberry wood is indicated by the BBC television programme *Antiques Roadshow*. This has run for over forty years and only one piece of mulberry furniture has ever featured in the programme – in 2009, at Bridlington, when Lennox Cato described a cabinet as being made of mulberry wood.[5]

There is an interesting characteristic of the wood in that when it is first felled and cut into planks it appears a very bright yellow. However, the wood is photosensitive and over time it develops into a rich 'nut' brown colour. Sometimes very large planks are available (from Europe and particularly Bulgaria) which can be 2 metres long. The wood can sometimes have complex figuring or burrs (Illustration 21) and in certain circumstances can have extremely unusual and highly regarded grain patterns, such as those seen in the island mulberry from Japan (see 'Sashimono, Kichizo and the Edo Tradition', below). In the United Kingdom some wood is called mulberry but is in actual fact other woods (for example, field maple, *Acer campestris*) which have been treated in specific ways, sometimes called 'mulberrying' (Illustration 22). This is discussed further in 'Coxed & Woster', below. This chapter focuses on the wood of the mulberry tree.

Generally speaking, most trees have to die in order to create material which is made into furniture and treen. In the case of the majority of mulberry trees this is by natural means when the trees die or fall over. In some circumstances wood can be used from major pruning – there are a number of examples in which owners of mulberry trees want to use the wood in some way because they are so emotionally attached to their tree. This is seen in the beautifully made desk (2009) by James Verner which used mulberry hexagonal oysters from pruned branches.

This chapter is divided into two key areas of inquiry. The first looks at the use of mulberry wood (or faux mulberry) in the United Kingdom and focuses on various techniques and technologies, with the company Titchmarsh & Goodwin playing a central role. Then there is a comparative view of the use of various mulberry woods in Japan, looking at the craft or sashimono tradition, with an emphasis on the maker and the diminishing marketplace. This chapter features the Japanese company Kichizo, which is a smaller concern than Titchmarsh & Goodwin but with a similar mission and age.

Trees and Treen

Mulberry wood in the United Kingdom is not easy to find commercially and the material has always been rare. Consequently, items made of genuine mulberry wood are also rare. Solid mulberry wood furniture is extremely scarce in the United Kingdom and in the main most furniture described as mulberry has a veneer (this will be discussed later). Smaller mulberry items, however, whether turned or carved, can be found and these are often termed treen. This is the generic name given to small items of wood. These have become very collectable and feature regularly in sales such as 'Treen for the Table', held on 8 November 2006, at Christie's, London, which included items from the Jonathan Levy collection.[6] The sale catalogue for this large collection showed no evidence of mulberry, though a variety of woods including box, yew and lignum vitae were included in what can be described as turned woodenware from the Elizabethan era to twentieth century. In the catalogue it says of Jonathan Levy: 'He described Treen collecting as

his hobby, which had its roots and inspiration in his interest in Trees and Woodland. He selected and planted many trees, with his family, at their country home in Buckinghamshire after the hurricane damage in 1987.' It appears that the collection included some pieces that had been previously owned by famous collectors such as John Fardon, W. J. Shepherd, Owen Evan-Thomas and Edward Pinto.

In fact, there is evidence of mulberry wood treen items in the collection of Edward Pinto which is now housed at Birmingham City Museums (the collection was sold to Birmingham in 1965 by Pinto who wanted a permanent home for his collections). The museum features certain items from the collection on the internet at the Birmingham Museums & Art Gallery Information Centre, with details of accession or museum numbers and relevant information (including illustrations). This collection is extremely comprehensive and features in two books by Pinto, one published in 1949 and a larger edition produced in 1969, entitled *Treen and Other Wooden Bygones: An Encyclopaedia and Social History*, which contains numerous illustrations of various items including a selection of the mulberry pieces. In the introduction Pinto indicates that the nucleus of the collection was gathered by Sir Ambrose Heal, who produced the book *The London Furniture Makers*[7] and was the founder of Heal's furniture/interiors stores

22 English Georgian 'mulberry' leaf tea caddy

23 English mulberry wood paper knife (detail) (Pinto Collection)

24 English Victorian mulberry wood knitting-wool container

(which still exist today). In addition, Pinto notes how technology has helped with his collection, citing carbon dating and stating: 'after the last war I was presented with a portion of an oak roof of the Middle Temple Hall, which was erected in the reign of Elizabeth I. I had three cigar caskets made from it. Radio carbon dating would have to declare the caskets as at least 400 years old'. Sections in the book consider mainly functional pieces relating to all aspects of life including eating, drinking, cleaning, writing and apothecary items.[8]

A visit to Birmingham City Museums to view the mulberry items revealed a range of objects made out of mulberry including an impressive decanter crafted from a single piece (Museum Number 1965T490) and a mulberry wood teapot (Museum Number 1965T3363) made by a Mr Pierce out of Shakespeare's mulberry (see below) and dated around 1765. Further smaller items include a teacup and saucer and various ephemera including a paper knife (Illustration 23). These will be discussed further in Chapter 5. There are just over a dozen items in the Pinto collection in mulberry wood out of many thousands of objects in the collection as a whole, which indicates the rarity of mulberry.

Examples of mulberry wood items in private collections are also rare, one such being described as 'functional folk art' – a wool storage vessel to aid in knitting (Illustration 24). The Pinto collection has an example of a similar item, but it is not made of mulberry wood.

There have been a number of treen-related articles in the BBC *Homes and Antiques* magazine, including one feature in 2007 that focused on kitchenalia that was shot on location at Dyrham Park.[9] The article recommends dealers specialising in wood and mentions Robert Hirschhorn. Another, later article with specific reference to treen recommends David Levi and Robert Young as dealers.[10] There is a growing and lucrative market in small wooden items and some can realise many thousands of pounds at auction. For example, a sale of the John Parry collection at Christie's featured a James I pear wood standing cup with an estimate of £4,000 to £6,000. The collection, comprising walnut, oak and yew, included an amazing array of fruitwood tea caddies and other treen, along with magnificent Georgian furniture.[11]

25 English mulberry wood salt bowl, by Cecil Jordan

26 English mulberry wood paper weight (apple form)

Titchmarsh & Goodwin

Titchmarsh & Goodwin is a well-established furniture manufacturing company that was founded in 1920 and celebrated its 90th anniversary in 2010. In their 2012 catalogue, *Fine English Furniture including the Georgian and Regency Period*, the company states:

> For over ninety years Titchmarsh & Goodwin have created beautiful furniture. Yet the roots of this family business go back to the eighteenth century, when around 1770, Samuel Goodwin, a carpenter from Woodbridge, Suffolk, sent his son George to join the workshops of a London cabinetmaker. On his return, with all the prestige of a London apprenticeship, George set himself up to design and create fine furniture.'[12]

Highly regarded contemporary makers such as Cecil Jordan (Illustration 25) occasionally use mulberry wood in their work, and unsigned mulberry wood items can also be found at amateur wood-turning craft fairs (Illustration 26).

It was 120 years later that the partnership between Titchmarsh & Goodwin was established and the Trinity Works at Ipswich were founded. Today the company includes a manufacturing team made up of a mix of craftspeople including cabinetmakers, turners and carvers,

27 English mulberry wood magazine table, by Titchmarsh & Goodwin

plus specialists in gilding, glazing, lacquer work and finishers (including French polishers).

The company's catalogue of furniture is impressive, and includes oak, mahogany and yew pieces ranging from small occasional tables (Illustrations 27 and 28) to massive case pieces including a breakfront library bookcase as featured in its Georgian and Regency period furniture catalogue.[13] The company takes great pride in the furniture it creates – a rigorous quality-control process is in place and pieces are crafted from wood using a combination of hand skills and appropriate design technology. The company has its own wood stores and responsibly sources all the wood it uses in manufacturing. In fact, it was instrumental in the formation of the Woodland Heritage charity and its wood always comes from approved United Kingdom and international sources. The company has an extensive archive of designs including over 20,000 perspective drawings with hand colouring (1920–1939) and a further 25,000 designs generated after the Second World War in its design studio. It is therefore able to offer a bespoke service and can also undertake modifications to any piece for clients. Many of the more popular designs feature in various high-quality catalogues relating to both historic periods and wood types.

In recent years the company has diversified and while the company's director Peter Goodwin was doing some preliminary research on mulberry furniture the Russian market was expanding. In order to cater for this the company started to develop furniture made out of Karelian birch veneers in the Russian Empire style. This wood has a very fancy and characteristic grain, and this development has proved a success with a separate catalogue. It was the intention of Peter Goodwin to create a special range to celebrate the company's 75th anniversary. This would involve the use of mulberry wood to produce a range of Coxed & Woster reproduction furniture. The mulberry project has a history that is recorded in the archives of Titchmarsh & Goodwin (1987–2007 approx.). This includes copious correspondence (both typed and handwritten, dated in or around 1988) with various antique dealers, including Norman Adams, Avon Antiques, Harvey & Co., Jonathon Harris, K. Chappell, John Keil, Apter–Fredericks and Great Brampton House Antiques for the purposes of information gathering in order to move the Goodwin mulberry project forward. Letters and replies appeared in other sources, including the *Antiques Trade*

28 English mulberry wood magazine table top

Gazette[14] and significantly also featured in a series of articles in *Woodland Heritage* in 2006, 2007 and 2008.[15]

Hurricane and Tempest

The hurricane of 1987 was important for Titchmarsh & Goodwin because it resulted in a significant number of large mulberry trees becoming available for processing into planks and veneer. No tree professionals or amateurs could forget this event if they had lived through it, and in Richard Mabey's book *Beechcombings: A Narrative of Trees*, the following has significance. In the Introduction, Mabey writes:

> At the height of the Great Storm of October 1987, with winds gusting up to 90 mph, a 38-metre-tall beech in a Kent garden lost its roothold and crashed through the roof of the adjoining house ... The

'hurricane', as it was popularly called, was the greatest natural cataclysm to hit north-west Europe for three hundred years. For those who experienced it first-hand it was an awesome and unforgettable reminder of the energy of nature. In less than five hours it caused billions of pounds worth of damage and toppled 15 million trees. Sevenoaks became one oak. The great park of Knole House in Kent lost a quarter of all its old oaks and beeches. At Chartwell, one-time home of Sir Winston Churchill, the dramatic horseshoe of beeches that topped the surrounding hills was simply wiped from the view.[16]

As might be expected, the hurricane not only destroyed much of the indigenous tree population in southern England but also felled some mulberry trees in usually sheltered garden sites. Peter Goodwin had a long-term interest in the mulberry tree because of the connection the wood has with furniture produced during the Georgian period, described as having a mulberry finish and often associated with the small firm of Coxed & Woster. The storm was an opportunity to collect felled trees in a green and ecological way in order to use the wood mainly for veneers for the development of a new range for Titchmarsh & Goodwin. Around twenty mulberry trees were sourced from various localities and these are recorded in the Titchmarsh & Goodwin archive, which includes details of mulberry tree material from the

Honourable Artillery Company, London, which was purchased for £100 in 1992. In addition to the money, the sellers also received small items made from the mulberry wood as mementos. Peter Goodwin decided at an early stage to offer owners a paperweight and paper knife made by the wood turner Richard Chapman (Illustration 29). This new source of a once rare wood is discussed in a 2006 *Woodland Heritage* article by Peter Goodwin:

> Trying to persuade owners to part with their mulberry trees was a complete waste of time. It seemed that these were so highly prized for their fruit and beautiful leaves that they were almost given revered status! All that changed on the night of 16th October when Michael Fish's renowned hurricane struck the south of England. Thousands of trees were blown down and hundreds of mulberry trees were lost. All of a sudden, I was being offered these 'untouchables'.[17]

Goodwin collected green wood from all over the south of England, including trees from London, Somerset, Berkshire and East Anglia from locations ranging from private residences to priories and halls (these are all recorded and listed in the archive, with tag numbers). Because he collected trees in person he heard many stories from the owners, which were often particularly focused on the trees' great age. When some of the trees were processed in the timber yard, and the annual rings counted, they appeared much younger (80 to 100 years

29 English mulberry wood paper knife and paperweight, by Richard Chapman

old). However, a letter from Peter Goodwin to Christopher Claxton Stevens (Norman Adams Ltd, the London antique dealers), dated 10 June 1988, states that some of the trees were between 150 and 200 years old.[18] One surprising feature of the trees was that they nearly all had considerable burrs and some of these were sent to Paris for traditional veneer cutting using sophisticated machinery (Illustration 28). In addition, some oysters were cut from the limbs (some of these were used in the creation of a tray in the collection of the Goodwin family). It was also Goodwin's intention to record sites of recovered mulberry trees and to include this information in the story of the furniture that was created from the wood – thus attaching a material culture to the final product.

His article continues by focusing on the story of Daniel Defoe and 'The Tempest of 1703': 'On the night of November 26th, a hurricane of frightening intensity struck, south of a line from Bristol to London … Thousands died and it was the worst disaster for the Royal Navy losing an entire fleet in that terrible night.' Goodwin then goes on to suggest a tentative connection between the two climatic events:

> After the 1703 Tempest, Coxed
> and Woster set about acquiring
> windblown black mulberry trees;
> just like us, some 284 years later,
> they could not use their carefully
> sawn butts and wet veneers until
> they had been slowly seasoned.
> Eventually, in about 1710, their
> wonderful burr mulberry furni-
> ture hit the market and stayed
> popular for about 10 years when
> their supplies dried up.

This statement is based on some fiction rather than actual fact, and was subsequently proved incorrect, which is rather disappointing. Throughout the article there is reference to the work by Edward Pinto on mulberry wood furniture in *Country Life*.[19] Pinto starts by stating:

> The black and white mulberry
> *Morus nigra* and *Morus alba*,
> provide reddish-brown heart-
> wood, rather like false acacia,
> and bright yellow sapwood. The
> timber is rarely available because
> even when there is no demand
> for the leaves for silkworms,
> mulberry trees are so esteemed
> for their luscious fruit that
> they are seldom cut down until
> in an advanced state of decay.
> John Evelyn in *Sylva*, refers to

> mulberry as 'a good bending
> wood for hoops and bows'.

The article essentially argues that much of the wood described as mulberry in case furniture is in fact maple, and Pinto concludes: 'however, none of it that I have seen – and I must have seen some hundreds of pieces over the past 40 to 50 years – is veneered in mulberry: all of it is maple'. Pinto also includes an illustration of mulberry burr from the collections of the Royal Botanic Garden, Kew, by way of a comparison, describing it as uninteresting – however, this is only one sample as there are examples of mulberry burr veneer which are lively and extensively patterned. The article includes illustrations of various pieces of antique furniture which have a complex figuring described as mulberry but which in Pinto's eyes are made of maple veneer. Others, including furniture historians, agree with Pinto, and a letter from the Building Research Advisory Service in the Titchmarsh & Goodwin archive (dated 22 August 1988) to Christopher Claxton Stevens indicated that a small veneer sample from a Coxed & Woster cabinet he sent for analysis was in fact *Acer* species rather than mulberry.

Mulberry Burr versus Maple Burr

Another article by Peter Goodwin discussing mulberry appeared in *Woodland Heritage* in 2007.[20] There is also a response to his 2006 article from Christopher Stevens. Claxton Stevens focuses on two points: 'I cannot comment on the quality of maple veneers, but I do encounter all over London as I travel, maples, sycamores and plane trees with wonderful looking burr growths. There is one particular type which tends to be a small tree, very prone to large burrs, and I wondered if this might be the field maple.' Secondly, 'Maple veneer is recorded on a number of occasions in the early eighteenth century, as being used but I am not aware of a single reference to mulberry, let alone burr mulberry, on furniture.' In a counter-argument, Peter Goodwin cites the work of the contemporary wood turner Richard Chapman (Illustration 30), with examples of evidence of both mulberry burr and field maple burr being exhibited in his work displayed at Norman Adams. Richard Chapman is a wood turner who has exhibited widely – at the Aldeburgh festival, for example, and he has also done work for the Royal Family, including a rose bowl to celebrate the 100th birthday of the Queen Mother. The conclusion Goodwin reaches is that the mulberry burr was more like the veneers in Coxed & Woster furniture. The debate continued, but a conclusion was

30 English mulberry wood wassail bowl, by Richard Chapman

objects, including small items such as snuff boxes (Illustrations 31 and 32) and medium items, including a tea caddy (Illustration 22). Coxed & Woster examples can be seen in various books such as *The Dictionary of English Furniture*,[21] and Ambrose Heal's *The London Furniture Makers*, which describes a piece as burr mulberry with kingwood bandings and pewter lines.[22] Pieces of furniture including bureaus have been described as mulberry and featured in auction house sales in the 1960s (Sotheby's, 1 November 1968, Lot 30), 1970s (Sotheby's, 5 October 1973, Lot 49) and 1980s (Christie's, 26 June 1986, Lot 97). In addition, a significant auction at The Refectory, Godalming, organised by Sotheby's, had a selection of burr items (some being described as mulberry), such as a Thomas Tompion longcase clock (estimate £40,000 to £50,000). The sale (27 and 28 June) was advertised in *Country Life*.[23] The British Museum has a similar mulberry clock (1695–1705) in its collections called Mulberry Tompion.[24] An item featured on the front cover of the December 1991/January 1992 edition of *Antique Collecting* was a mulberry item (Lot 105) in a sale taking place at Bonham's, London. A piece described as a George I pewter-inlaid field maple and kingwood cabinet was exhibited at the Grosvenor House fair in 2008 and the dealers Apter–Fredericks described a bureau bookcase as being made of burr maple. On their website it stated:

> It is interesting that, although this piece is too good to be by the celebrated firm of Coxed & Woster, it exhibits a feature that this partnership has almost made its own. That is, the use of field or burr maple, chemically altered to encourage the wood and a mulberried finish to resemble tortoise-shell.

reached with some scientific work and evidence from Adam Bowett that seems to indicate that the mulberry furniture was actually veneered with field maple (*Acer campestris*).

Some large auction houses still recognise the descriptive term 'mulberry'. For example, Lyon & Turnbull (established 1826) of Edinburgh recorded some 'mulberry' pieces but they are still relatively rare – from 2000 to 2007 they only had six items with the descriptor mulberry, including a mulberry wood apple-shaped tea caddy, which was part of the Lord Constantine collection (Lot 163). The term has been extensively used in the antiques trade for Georgian

31 English Georgian 'mulberry' wood round snuff box

More-recent publications also feature photographs of Coxed/Coxed & Woster case pieces, including *English Furniture, 1660–1714* by Adam Bowett.[25] A subsequent volume, *Early Georgian Furniture, 1715–1740*, has illustrated information on John Coxed, Grace Coxed and Thomas Woster.[26] Thus it would appear that opinions have firmly changed and that for accuracy's sake the term maple should be used, although romantically it must be so much more satisfying to own a piece of 'mulberry' furniture.

Coxed & Woster

An article in the 2008 edition of *Woodland Heritage* concluded the 'mulberry' debate, with information in the main provided again by Adam Bowett, in which he reviewed the available material and summarised his findings.[27] Using technological analysis with microscopy he concluded that not one piece of Coxed & Woster furniture produced in the early eighteenth century could be confirmed as being made from mulberry wood. The company was associated with the White Swan in St Paul's churchyard, London. In fact, a small sample of furniture labels which feature the white swan exist, sometimes with just John Coxed's name mentioned and at other times with G. Coxed and T. Woster appearing together in partnership. It would seem that the partnership started in 1710 and lasted just over a dozen years, although the total productive period of the group is cited as being from 1690 to 1736 (Thomas Woster died in 1736). There was a fashion in Europe at the time for brass-inlaid tortoiseshell-veneered furniture after the French Royal cabinetmaker André Charles Boulle (1642–1732). There was probably an attempt by Coxed & Woster to reproduce this

in inexpensive materials that were available locally, such as pewter and field maple.

It would appear that they created a tortoiseshell finish by treating field maple (and possibly other species) with chemicals. A method described in 1688 in a *Treatise on Japanning and Varnishing* suggested a treatment of nitric acid (*Aqua fortis*) and the application of heat. The wood turned bright yellow as a result, and then a further application of a lampblack oil emulsion could be wiped over the yellow surface. This resulted in varied penetration of the stain and created a mottled tortoiseshell appearance. In addition, it would also appear that field maple was highly regarded as a wood by John Evelyn (1664), Batty Langley (1720s), J. C. Loudon (1838) and John Selby Prideaux (1842). In an article in the journal *Regional Furniture*, Adam Bowett writes:

> The 'Mapell' (*Acer campestris*), of which Lazarus Stiles had 72 pieces in his workshop in 1724, was probably also in burr form. It may have been stained in colours; the best known exponents of stained burr maple veneers were John Coxed and his successors, Grace Coxed and Thomas Woster, but there were undoubtedly others.[28]

In his 2008 *Woodland Heritage* article, the same author concludes: 'The mythology of mulberry as a furniture wood seems to have emerged in the latter part of the nineteenth century, with a number of writers suggesting that the wood of both *M. alba* and *M. nigra* was used in cabinet work.'[29] He goes on: 'The association of mulberry with early eighteenth century cabinet making, and specifically with the London firm of Coxed & Woster (1711–1735), is a purely twentieth century phenomenon.' He gives the example of an article about mulberry furniture in *Apollo* (1941) – 'The Work of Coxed & Woster in Mulberry Wood and Burr Elm' – as the source of the myth. He concludes:

> Since then the myth of 'mulberry wood' has served the antiques trade well, but in recent years responsible dealers and auctioneers have begun to abandon the term in favour of 'stained field maple'. This is a step in the direction of historical truth, but it covers a number of different woods whose true identities we are only beginning to discover. However, they all have at least this in common – none of them is burr mulberry.

It was disappointing for Peter Goodwin on a personal level and for the company Titchmarsh & Goodwin that the mulberry project could not be fulfilled. Because the company is concerned with historical accuracy and truth it felt that it could not have an incorrect wood veneer on Coxed & Woster reproductions. It does occasionally use mulberry veneer on pieces such as the small table featured in Illustration 27 and a mahogany Empire kneehole desk with mulberry detail which is in their *Fine English Furniture including the Georgian and Regency Period* catalogue.[30] However, another company specialising in high-quality reproduction furniture, Arthur Brett, does produce a burr elm chest of drawers with a 'mulberry' finish and the catalogue can be viewed on a compact disc. A further article in *Woodland Heritage* in 2009 focused on mulberry wood usage in Japan and it is this subject to which we will now turn.[31]

Japanese Furniture and Mulberry Wood

Like furniture in the United Kingdom, furniture produced in Japan is generally classified by history and then functional type. The history is detailed in Kazuko Koizumi's book *Traditional Japanese Furniture: A Definitive Guide*,[32] and a simple subdivision includes categories such as Ancient, Medieval, Pre-Modern, Early Modern and Modern. Mulberry wood pieces feature throughout, including sixteenth-century examples, and tend to use mulberry wood sourced from *Morus alba* species. In Japan there are specific pieces of furniture which are considered essential for the home and representative of the culture. These are:

1. The tansu. This is often made of paulownia and used for storage of textiles and other items.[33] There is a story that every father with a daughter will plant a paulownia seed in his garden so that a tansu can be made out of the wood when she marries.

2. The hibachi. Often made of zelkova with copper and used as a heat source by the addition of charcoal. One example is discussed and illustrated in the catalogue *The Art of Japanese Craft: 1875 to Present*, edited by Felice Fischer.[34] Gian Carlo Calza's book *Japan Style* features a classic hibachi in the famous anonymous photograph 'Tea Time in Japan' circa 1900.[35] A 1920s autochrome photograph showing a Japanese Royal Family interior places the hibachi in context in a traditional reception room.[36] The Japanese Royal Family will be mentioned later in the context of shimakuwa mulberry.

3. The cha-dansu. This tea chest is often made of mulberry wood (Illustration 33, labelled 3). Mulberry wood, like cherry wood, is light-sensitive and in *Traditional Japanese Furniture* it states: 'Mulberry wood characteristically deepens in colour and glow over the years, hence its frequent use for bridal trousseau furnishings, the folk-wisdom running that it will "age beautifully with the women"'.[37]

Mulberry wood features in many furniture types, including case pieces or cabinetry, as well as a multitude of smaller items such as study and writing paraphernalia including writing boxes/suzuri-baco (Illustration 34), toiletry accessories such as mirrors (Illustration 35) and items related to tobacco (Illustration 36) and the tea ceremony (Illustrations 37 and 38). The main difference in furniture forms is the fact that in Japanese culture people tend to sit on the floor, and this obviously influences the scale and design of furniture pieces.

Mulberry wood in Japan has a complex taxonomy and can essentially be divided into three types. The first is the lowest quality, is often stained a dark brown and is frequently used for standard pieces including storage boxes and clothes racks. This type of mulberry can also have a lime-washed appearance, as seen in Illustrations 39 and 40. A lime wash can also be applied as a preparatory process in the creation of shimakuwa or island mulberry pieces.[38] The second type is of better quality and is often described as mountain mulberry and can have a very fancy moiré grain as featured in the sewing box/hari-bako (Illustration 41) and the tobacco

33 Japanese tea ceremony room furniture and fixtures made of mulberry wood

1

2

3

4

5

6

7

34 Japanese mulberry
writing box in shimakuwa,
by Toshio Shimazaki

35 Japanese mulberry
small mirror in
shimakuwa, by Tadashi
Kimura

36 Japanese mulberry
wood tobacco box

37 Japanese mulberry
wood tea utensil storage
box

38 Japanese mulberry wood thin green tea container

box/tabako-bon, which has a burled mulberry grain on the front surface (Illustration 36). Finally, and significantly for this study, there is island mulberry, which is normally produced on Hachijojima, Miyakejima and Mikurajima – islands off the Izu peninsula that can be accessed from Tokyo by either boat or plane.[39] Island mulberry is a specific species of *Morus alba* and is called *Morus kagayamae* Koidz, and is generally termed shimakuwa. The wood from this species is of the finest quality, can have very complex grain systems and is characterised by its golden colour. The wood is described in the book *Tokyo no shima*,[40] where we read:

> Then finally, a shimakuwa writing desk and a shogi box appeared. When I picked up the box and turned it around, it kept changing its impressions phantasmagorically, gleaming under the electric light. From inside the wooden board which ought to be flat, it was gleaming as if golden waves were drifting about or gathering clouds playing with sunlight.

The raw material is featured in Illustrations 42 and 43 and shows both the inner grain and outer appearance of the bark on the tree. A finished item in the form of an individual writing box/suzuri-baco is featured in Illustration 34.

Beyond the Izu islands are the Bonin islands, which also have some mulberry trees that produce wood called Ogasawara kuwa. Some of the trees are rumoured to be 2,000 years old. The islands themselves are a UNESCO world heritage site and are described as the Galapagos Islands of the Orient (also see Charles Darwin, in Chapter 5, below). In *Traditional Japanese Furniture*, we read:

> Furniture grade wood must ... be obtained from completely wild trees, the finest of which are said to come from Okura and Miyake islands off Izu peninsula. Some of these trees are between five hundred and a thousand years old. Unsurpassed for their rich and intricate grain, they possess a natural glow that is highly prized.[41]

39 Japanese mulberry
wood tea utensil storage
box

40 Japanese mulberry
wood tea utensils

41 Japanese mulberry wood sewing box

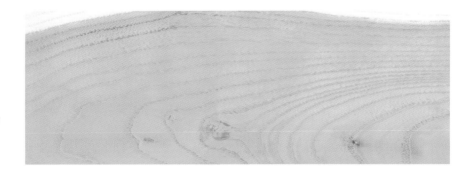

42 Japanese raw mulberry wood (shimakuwa) from the Izu Islands (internal)

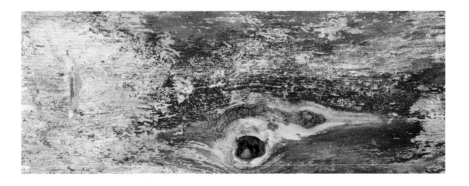

43 Japanese raw mulberry wood (shimakuwa) from the Izu Islands (external)

For the commemoration of Emperor Showa's enthronement, eight giant shimakuwa trees were removed from Mikurajima, with some difficulty because of the terrain. They were thought to be over 1,000 years old. Indeed, it is this wood which established the sashimono tradition in Japan during the Edo period (1600–1868), and it continues to be highly regarded and used in contemporary Japan. The Edo sashimono-shi maker Akira Watanabe, whenever asked about the best wood for making furniture, invariably says shimakuwa, because it glows and gleams. The Sailor pen company recently celebrated its 100th anniversary by producing a limited edition shimakuwa fountain pen (Illustration 44), which is contained in an impressive maki-e black lacquer box by Kosen Oshita. The pen is covered in an urushi lacquer, which tends to be the finish of choice for most makers of shimakuwa items. The best urushi comes from the Joubou-ji area of northern Japan. Urushi is the traditional finish for wood and has a very extensive history. It comes from the sap of the tree *Rhus verniciflua* (also known as *Toxicodendron verniciflum*), which is a member of the sumac family. The application of lacquer is a complex and skilled process often completed by specialists called urushiya or lacquerers.[42] Contemporary craft makers (not sashimono) occasionally use shimakuwa for prestigious items for Japanese businessmen, including a business card holder (Illustration 45) and a boxed pair of chopsticks (Illustration 46), sold by the Sakamoto Otozo Shoten Co., which is located in Fukushima prefecture.

44 Japanese mulberry wood limited edition Sailor pen in shimakuwa

45 Japanese business card holder in shimakuwa

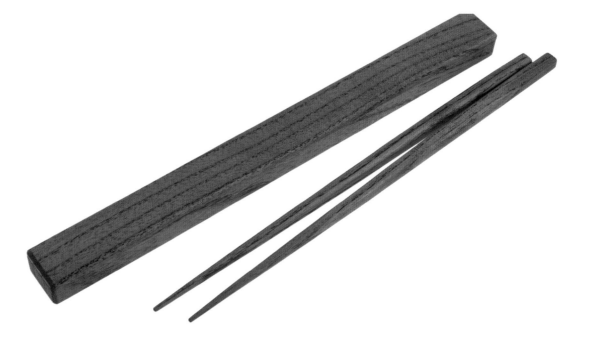

46 Japanese mulberry chopsticks and box in shimakuwa

Sashimono, Kichizo and the Edo Tradition

Kichizo, like Titchmarsh & Goodwin in the United Kingdom, is a company that manufactures furniture with a strong and established tradition. Kichizo is a small company with a workshop in Shizuoka, Shizuoka prefecture, which is geographically close to the Izu peninsula, separated only by Suragu Bay, and also in close proximity to Tokyo. The company has a small number of employees or makers who mainly craft furniture by hand. It was established in 1922 and is a family-run firm, presently managed by Yoshitaka Sugiyama, who is the president. His grandfather, Kichizo Sugiyama, started an independent business and his father, Seiichi Sugiyama, founded the company as it exists today. All communications with Yoshitaka and Kichizo have to be made via Kakeshi Uchimura at Sumitomo Bakelite Company, Tokyo because no one at Kichizo can speak English. The company is celebrating its 90th anniversary and produces a number of different ranges including Saranban and Tougudo, which they retail at various Tokyo department stores. The furniture is grouped in collections including mainly classical pieces such as a Li Dynasty Korean range (production started in 1983) and a sashimono mulberry collection (started in 1970). The name sashimono comes from the word for ruler (monosashi) because of the reputation the furniture makers have for extreme accuracy.

The company utilises solid woods and veneers, and uses wood varieties outside the normal scope of the European tradition, including paulownia, zelkova and island mulberry. Furniture ranges include folding screens, lighting, tables, chairs and settees as well as case furniture. A sample of Kichizo mulberry sashimono pieces are illustrated in this book, including a sewing cabinet, vanity cabinet, tissue box and waste paper box (Illustrations 47, 48, 49 and 50). The most notable difference between the furniture Kichizo produces and the European tradition is the scale of the work. Japanese furniture is much smaller than you would expect if you are used to normal-sized pieces in the United Kingdom.

The Kichizo company is famous for its range of Zen shrines, Buddhist worship pieces and Zushi altars (Illustration 51), which it produces in various woods and in some cases in veneer with a contemporary urethane finish (rather than a urushi finish). Some of the pieces in the collections have a remarkably contemporary appearance and this includes a number of the mulberry pieces. The mulberry collection is made in the sashimono tradition but the company does use glue and fixings such as screws in its work, so the sashimono tradition is not completely upheld. Sashimono featured in a Japanese television programme, *Begin Japanology*, presented by Peter Barakan.[43] The programme featured the craftsmen and the tradition of making furniture out of wood without any glue or nails and screws – although metal handles and other dressings (made by specific makers called chokinya) are used.

The skill encountered in authentic sashimono craftsmen is incomparable and the workers in such a tradition have a

47 Japanese mulberry
wood sewing cabinet in
shimakuwa, by Kichizo

considerable apprenticeship over many years. An important part of working the woods involves the woodworking tools, which are works of art in themselves and should be made by the craftsmen. Sometimes workers in the sashimono tradition can have over 150 planes and hundreds of razor-sharp tools, including chisels. The craftsmen use materials outside the general scope of the British tradition. For example, in shimakuwa mulberry pieces the wood is not finished using glass paper or sandpaper but with a leaf from the Muku tree – *Aphananthe aspera*. The leaves are gathered in the autumn and carefully dried and then used to create a very fine lustre on the wood. The art of the craftsmen means that they can make three-dimensional invisible joints which in effect piece together like a jigsaw.[44] The dove-tail joints are so rigorously made that they form watertight connections by simply tapping two interlocking pieces together – the level of accuracy can be less than one tenth of a millimetre. There are a variety of different joints the makers can utilise, including hagiawase (butted joints), kumitsugi (box joints) and hozoguni (tenon joints). In Elizabeth Kiritani's *Vanishing Japan*,

these sashimono makers are called Edo-style joiners because they first developed their skills during the Edo period in Japan and have a significant place in Japans furniture history:

> In the twelfth century special artisans called hakotsukuribe formed a guild that made platforms for futon, portable Chinese chests, folding tables, and other furnishings used by the Imperial Court, the nobility, and the feudal lords. The Momoyama period in the latter half of the sixteenth century brought a long interval of peace, and with it, a renaissance that included elaborate furniture and things made of wood.[45]

As an apparent reaction to this, Edo sashimono, or Edo woodworking, developed and evolved to become the essence of restraint. The Monoyama period ran from 1568 to 1600 while the Edo period continued directly after (1600–1868). It was incredibly important for the developing indigenous Arts and Crafts movement in Japan and was probably the most productive in its history. The Edo period, under the banner

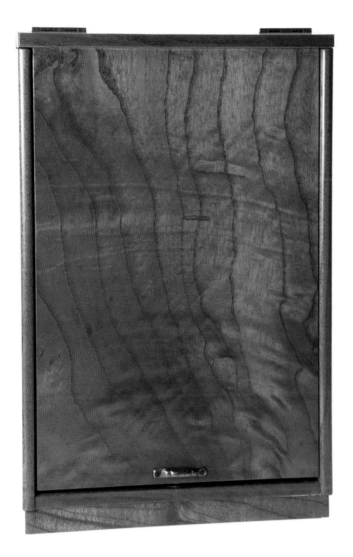

49 Japanese mulberry
wood tissue box in
shimakuwa, by Kichizo

48 Japanese mulberry
wood vanity cabinet in
shimakuwa, by Kichizo

50 Japanese mulberry
wood waste paper box in
shimakuwa, by Kichizo

'samurai, court and townspeople', is featured in the Mitsubishi Corporation Japanese galleries at the British Museum. Edo furniture encompassed developing items for merchants and the warrior classes (shogunate). By the early part of the 1700s, there were over a million people living in Edo and this made it the largest city in the world – the sashimono makers had a ready market for their wares. In the modern Meiji period (1868–1912), Edo was renamed Tokyo and the city has continued to develop through both the Taisho, Showa and Heisei periods.

As well as artistic practices such as the Kabuki theatre, the Imperial Court required wood items (Illustration 52). Shimakuwa mulberry has always been associated with the Japanese Royal Family and there are two extant examples of this. The royal train was lined with shimakuwa mulberry on the enthronement of Emperor Taisho (r.1879–1926), and there are shimakuwa furnishings in the Hayama Imperial villa in Kanagawa prefecture that were given to celebrate Emperor Showa's enthronement (r.1926–1989). In *A History of the World in 100*

Objects, Neil MacGregor selected an Edo image in the form of a print (in the floating world aesthetic) entitled *The Great Wave (off Kanagawa)*, made around 1830.[46] It is one from a series of 36 views of Mount Fuji by Katsushika Hokusai, and MacGregor declared it a decorative image of timeless Japan. Much of sashimono furniture is timeless in its aesthetic, and the reason is that it developed in the Edo taste, which was characterised by a lack of decoration and ostentatious elements.

The most significant aspect of sashimono work is the wood, which the makers precisely inspect so that they can develop their sophisticated jointing systems around the intrinsic strength of the wood – they work with the grain rather than against it. This in part is recognised in iki – a Japanese word which relates to elegance, simplicity and, most importantly, refinement. The best sashimono furniture, and particularly that in shimakuwa mulberry, must surely be the most outstanding in the world. It is also becoming the most expensive – a single piece of high-quality shimakuwa lumber today can cost as much as 700,000 yen (£3,700), while in 1995 the market for raw Mikurajima mulberry logs was an astonishing 87,000,000 yen. A detailed account of island mulberry is featured in *Islands of Tokyo*.[47] Because of the long apprenticeships and the passing of skills from one generation to the next, the sashimono tradition is dying out in Japan. There are a multitude of reasons for this, the main one being that the furniture is classed as heirloom and can be very expensive. Recently, a tray by Soumei Maeda in

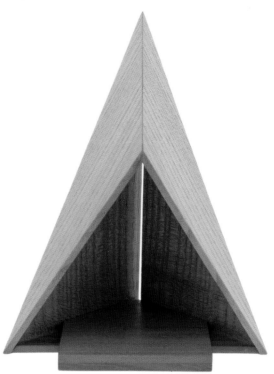

51 Japanese mulberry wood portable altar in shimakuwa, by Kichizo

a Japanese version of the television programme *Antiques Roadshow* was valued at around a million yen.

As in the rest of the world, IKEA and MUJI have become a force in the Japanese marketplace and sadly very few people appreciate sashimono furniture enough to buy it. The proponents of the sashimono tradition of furniture are growing older and many have died, unable to pass their skills on to the next generation.

52 Japanese mulberry wood seat in shimakuwa, by Tadashi Kimura

53 Japanese mulberry
wood hand mirror
in shimakuwa, by
Tadashi Kimura

One such is Ono Showasai (1912–1996) whose beautiful mulberry and mottled persimmon box (1993) was featured in the British Museum exhibition *Crafting Beauty in Modern Japan.*[48] Ono Showasai was famous for using complex figured mulberry grains such as that described as 'grape burl' and he had previously appeared in a V&A publication, *Japanese Studio Crafts Tradition and the Avant-Garde,*[49] in which his exquisitely modulated and graduated mulberry wood oblong containers with persimmon and box banding are illustrated. He was awarded the designation of 'national living treasure' (ningen kokuho) in 1984, a status the government awards to people whom it considers to be important repositories of tangible knowledge and skill, which was instigated in 1950 under a law for the protection of cultural properties. Other makers are also aging, like Toshio Toda (born 1951), who features in *Vanishing Japan.*[50] Toshio Toda became an apprentice in the sashimono tradition at the age of 18 and after a long apprenticeship (seven years) with Kuniharu Shimazaki the first thing he was allowed to make on his own was a pair of chopsticks. The book records a visit to his workshop at Naegishi:

> Mr Toda sat cross legged on a wooden workshop floor in front of the dresser that he was crafting. His walls are littered with handmade tools and corners are piled with large pieces of wood

drying. Outside the house, too, there are stacks of wood, carefully protected from the sun and rain, drying. To prevent his furniture from warping, he will dry his wood from two to thirty years. Favoured wood has beautiful grain; mulberry, pear, Japanese cedar, paulownia, or zelkova.

Toshio Toda specialises in mulberry work, making the most beautiful trays and smaller items such as a mirror in shimmering island mulberry. There are still around a dozen companies in Japan producing objects in wood that can be classed in the sashimono tradition. A number of these have been named national living treasures. There are centres such as Kigakuan that display and sell the work of sashimono makers in the Yanaka district of Tokyo. The work of Toshio Toda is displayed there but the prices attached to some pieces can be a shock for those who have no idea of the effort and skill which goes into each piece – a pair of mulberry chopsticks can cost £500.

Kichizo still works with the island mulberry because in the main it is used as veneer rather than in solid form, and while the veneered furniture is expensive it is still affordable. However, solid shimakuwa mulberry furniture with spectacular grain patterns can cost many millions of yen and some sashimono craftsmen who use mulberry wood are diversifying and have

54 Japanese mulberry
wood frame made from
shimakuwa, by Toshio
Shimazaki

established an Internet presence, with furniture makers such as Tadao Haji, Kokichi Oobuchi and Tadashi Kimura being represented.[51] Tadashi Kimura was born in 1938 in Hiroshima prefecture and started his apprenticeship in the Western Furniture Manufacturing Company before moving to Kyoto at the age of 18 so that he could be taught by the master craftsman Kuniharu Shimazaki, who was an authority in bijutsu sashimono. Tadashi Kimura has since specialised in large island mulberry (shimakuwa) case pieces alongside smaller items (e.g., Illustration 53). Unfortunately, he now only uses the Miyakejima island mulberry

infrequently because it has become so difficult to obtain, opting instead for yellow birch (*Betula alleghaniensis*). Finally, there are a number of artisans with the name Shimazaki that are associated with shimakuwa mulberry, including the maker of various items (Illustrations 54, 55 and 56) who was called Toshio Shimazaki.

Sashimono, Shimakuwa and the Izu Islands

Perhaps the most famous of the Izu islands with regard to mulberry trees is Mikurajima.[52] It is an area of outstanding scientific interest and beauty. The island has some full-time woodland

55 Japanese mulberry
wood thin green tea
container in shimakuwa,
by Toshio Shimazaki

56 Japanese mulberry
wood thin green tea
container, tray and
scoop in shimakuwa

guides who show visitors around the terrain (for a small charge). In 2004, regulations were introduced that mean that people cannot be unaccompanied in the mountain forest areas. These include impressive forestation comprising *Castanopsis sieboldii* (Akazawa giant trees), *Machilus thunbergii*, *Dendropanax trifidus*, *Buxus microphylla* and *Morus kagayamae* – the island mulberry. The rich flora is accompanied by an equally rich fauna, including woodpeckers, robins and the streaked shearwater *Calonectris leucomelas*. This bird is, in part, responsible for the luxuriant vegetation, which includes a rich ecosystem of camellias, angelica, epiphytic ferns and numerous rare wild flowers, through its depositing droppings across the island. A guide, Hirose Noriyoshi, suggests that the island 'floats' in the Pacific Ocean and lies within the Kuroshio current, which influences the island's climate. The island terminates on all sides in sheer cliffs except for one natural harbour and is almost entirely covered in very deep forests and vegetation.

The mulberry from Mikurajima is very highly regarded and is the most prized material for the manufacture of furniture and smaller items (see Illustrations 57, 58, 59, 60, 61 and 62). Mikurajima is one of the islands which form the Izu archipelago – a very active volcanic series which regularly appears on seismic activity monitoring.[53] Mikurajima is approximately 20 kilometres from the other famous mulberry island Miyakejima and is a relatively small island with an area of approximately 20 square kilometres. At the centre of the island is Mount Oyama, which is just over 850 metres high, and this area is totally unpopulated. The majority of the slightly fewer than 300 islanders live by the sea in the harbour area and the main occupation is fishing and tourism. Another lucrative crop from the island is boxwood, which produces beautiful material for the manufacture of combs and seals, as well as the highest-quality chess pieces (shogi). This trade has been evident since the Edo period and continues alongside the harvesting of shimakuwa mulberry.

57 Japanese mulberry wood leaf tea container in shimakuwa, by Shouji Furukawa

58 Japanese mulberry wood chopstick rests and box in shimakuwa, by Toshio Shimazaki

In the Edo period, since the artisans responsible for using island mulberry wood were the most experienced and highly regarded, they were awarded the special title Kuwamonoshi. Yoshitaka Sugiyama, the president of Kichizo, writes:

> The mulberry material that grows naturally in Izu islands Miyakejima and Mikurajima is [called] 'island mulberry'. [The colour and feel of the wood] were liked, and valued highly as [the] highest peak of 'Edo joinery' by the Edo people who respected chic ... the workman who produces the joinery furniture of the island mulberry is called, 'Kuwamonoshi', and has been revered.[54]

A particularly renowned practitioner of his craft was Soumei Maeda (and. interestingly, the Japanese characters for his name mean 'bright

61 Japanese mulberry wood incense container in shimakuwa, by Toshio Shimazaki

mulberry tree'). He lived on Miyake Island and passed on the heritage to a series of Edo-style master carpenters, including Kuniharu Shimasaki and Tadashi Kimura. In a translated interview, Tadashi Kimura explained why island mulberry is so special for craftspeople. He suggests that the wood is a delight to work because:

> The colour and the sheen are really different, even when you plane it. The mulberry from the mainland is called local mulberry, but if it is left standing over a long period it becomes discoloured all the way through. Island mulberry, however, loses its colour only very slowly. When the outside goes brown, even dark brown, if you plane it the golden yellow colour comes through.

The golden colour is termed Kuwairo, which can be translated as a light yellow mulberry blossom colour. The wood is hard, rarely warps and has great flexibility, but perhaps its most important virtue is the grain. At its best the grain can be separated into two characters – the first looks like sand ripples on a beach, while

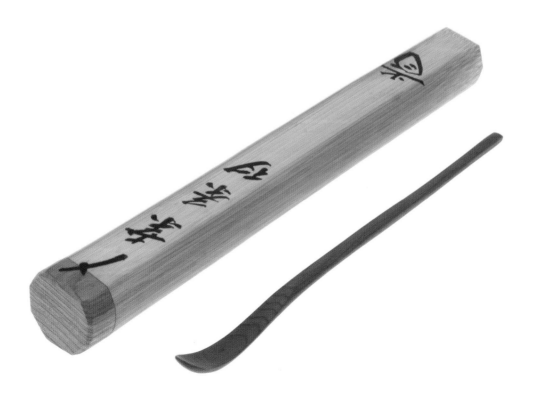

62 Japanese mulberry wood tea scoop in shimakuwa with bamboo case

the second is the floating grain that appears to be like waves or ripples in the sea or a rock pool when a stone is dropped in (Illustration 48). It is this three-dimensional feature of the best shimakuwa that makes it unique and very expensive. Some observers have compared it to the semi-precious chatoyant gemstone tigerseye in that it has a highly reflective quality which shifts with the light. Artisans who use the wood have described the grain as 'having silver in it' and 'coming and going', and even evoking the image of a calm water's surface which glows in the morning or evening sun. These characteristics are termed Ittekoi in Japanese, which amongst other things relates to the symmetry of the grain.

The difficulty in obtaining shimakuwa is likely to continue and could even get worse because the mulberry trees appear to be dying on Mikurajima. This could be for a number of reasons relating to the volcanicity of the islands but is also possibly due to climate change – at the present time scientists are looking into the reasons why. Virtually all the easily accessible wood has been harvested on the islands and the trees in many cases are very small and not suitable for use. However, wood is provided for specialist craftsman who have to use island-sourced mulberry. One such example is Fushiki Ishida, who is a highly skilled maker of the Japanese lute (Biwa) that is used for ceremonial music-making, including in the Imperial Court. Fushiki Ishida is a fourth-generation artisan who was born in 1937 in Aomori prefecture but is now based in the Toranomon district of Tokyo. He is passing on his skills to his eldest son Katsuyoshi and they are virtually the only people in Japan still making Satsuma Biwa. In 2003, he received an official commendation from the chief of the cultural affairs agency and in 2006 was formally recognised as a designated holder of selected skills requiring preservation by the Japanese government. He too has been named a national living treasure. Island mulberry is used for the instruments because it gives a special sound, and along with zelkova is the main wood of construction. The shimakuwa wood is also selected for its natural beauty and on occasion decorated with maki-e lacquer similar to that used for Namiki pens.[55] Maki-e is another refined process in which multiple layers of lacquer are applied along with gold and silver particles to create decorative effects. The most complex maki-e patterns can take several months to complete, a process illustrated in Nick Foulkes and Charles March's book *Dunhill by Design*.[56]

James Bond

A final note is required on Miyakejima, which has a chequered recent history because of its volcanic activity. At the turn of the millennium, in 2000, the strato volcano, called Oyama, like that on Mikurajima, started to erupt, which meant that the island had to be fully evacuated. It was not until 2005 that residents were allowed to return to the island with the proviso that they wear gas masks whenever an alarm bell rings on the island. The noxious sulphuric gases remain a hazard and the island has some of the highest recorded levels in the world. The island is therefore not unlike that in the James Bond film *You Only Live Twice*,[57] and was possibly the prototype for the fictional island. This was previously suggested in an article in the 2009 *Woodland Heritage* journal.[58] Like Mikurajima, the island is famous for its flora and fauna and is a source of shimakuwa. During the Edo period the island was also used as a penal colony. Hence, as at Wakefield in the United Kingdom, the mulberry tree is associated with a prison.

Conclusion

This chapter is a tale of two companies in two culturally different countries, the United Kingdom and Japan. Essentially, however, the techniques and making practices are the same – fundamentally based around skill and craft. The furniture is hand finished and the materials used are the best quality (with sustainable sourcing and truth to materials), whether veneer or solid wood. With specific reference to mulberry, the differences become apparent when the raw material is compared. In the United Kingdom, when something is described as mulberry it is generally not made of *Morus* species wood but of material derived from a number of different tree species, the applied surface being faux mulberry and the process described as 'mulberrying'. In Japan, mulberry does come from *Morus* species and the wood is called kuwa – hence the term shimakuwa. Sadly, in both countries the companies are struggling to make sustainable profits because of the economic climate and changes in fashion. In the United Kingdom at the moment there is little demand for 'brown' furniture in the antique trade, and there is bound to be a consequent downturn in the reproduction antique marketplace. This is what Titchmarsh & Goodwin excel in and their back catalogue is impressive and based on our furniture heritage. They offer a really good alternative for people who want a particular furniture piece but cannot afford the original. The situation with Kichizo is similar in that it offers quality pieces when the originals are no longer available. Both companies offer a bespoke service. They have tried to create alternatives in what is a complex and moving international marketplace and use new technologies to achieve this – whether it be Internet promotion or computer-aided design. In the Winterthur catalogue, *Seeing Things Differently*, it states:

> Although much of what was produced in the colonial period was 'bespoke' work (that is, made to satisfy a specific order), wares 'readymade after the newest fashion' became increasingly available in urban areas after the mid eighteenth century. All of these participants combined to form a marketplace that, although different from today's, has many striking similarities and offers significant insight into early decorative arts and the forces that shaped them.[59]

Titchmarsh & Goodwin and Kichizo have been established for a significant period and have a heritage that is worth keeping. The major problem that both companies face is the trend for 'throwaway' fashion furniture, which was epitomised by IKEA's 1996 'Chuck Out Your Chintz' television campaign, with its slogan 'Fight chintz oppression with bold self-expression'.[60] There could be no more diametrically opposed pieces of furniture than an IKEA Billy bookcase and a shimakuwa display cabinet by Kichizo. The insidious influence of IKEA has sadly reached Japan and the cultural counterpoints of furniture are lost in the Swedish-inspired infiltration into Japanese interiors.[61] Using a shimakuwa analogy, perhaps the tide is changing and the hope is that Titchmarsh & Goodwin along with Kichizo will survive and prosper when people realise that quality is important and that the most sustainable furniture is that which can be passed on from generation to generation.

Notes to Chapter 3

1 Maureen Butler, *Gordon Russell: Vision and Reality* (Broadway: Gordon Russell Museum, 2007).

2 Private handwritten correspondence from Ray Leigh dated 2 February 2008. This was on letterheaded paper from the Gordon Russell Museum, which was followed by a letter on 28 February 2008 from Trevor Chinn (Trustee) detailing the mulberry piece, with attached plans and photographs.

3 Email correspondence dated 5 February 2008 to the author from Adam Bowett.

4 Adam Bowett, *English Furniture, 1660–1714 from Charles II to Queen Anne* (Woodbridge: The Antique Collectors' Club, 2002). The quotation is taken from the Appendix on p. 310.

5 *Antiques Roadshow*, series 31, episodes 24 and 25, first broadcast on BBC1 television in 2009.

6 Auction catalogue entitled *Treen for the Table* (2006). This included items from the Jonathan Levy collection sale which took place on 8 November at Christie's, London.

7 Sir Ambrose Heal, *The London Furniture Makers: From the Restoration to the Victorian Era, 1660–1840* (New York: Dover Publications, 1953).

8 Edward H. Pinto, *Treen and Other Wooden Bygones: An Encyclopaedia and Social History* (London: G. Bell & Sons, 1969), p. 5.

9 Juliet Pospielovsky, 'A Serving of Tradition', *BBC Homes and Antiques*, January 2007, pp. 84–89.

10 Katrina Burroughs, 'One Good Turn', *BBC Homes and Antiques*, March 2006, pp. 43–49.

11 Auction catalogue entitled *John Parry Collection* (2010) produced for a sale held on 25 March at Christie's, London. The standing cup is shown on p. 3 and the fruitwood tea caddies appear on pp. 44–49.

12 Furniture catalogue *Fine English Furniture including the Georgian and Regency Period* (2012) produced by Titchmarsh & Goodwin, Suffolk in a section entitled 'The Roots of a Suffolk Company'.

13 Ibid., p. 53.

14 Peter Goodwin gave access to the Titchmarsh & Goodwin (and Goodwin) archive referencing the complete mulberry project, including letters and papers, and cuttings from the *Antiques Trade Gazette*.

15 *Woodland Heritage* is a yearly publication produced by the Woodland Heritage charity whose chairman is Peter Goodwin. Publications from 2006, 2007, 2008 and 2009 were used for this study.

16 Richard Mabey, *Beechcombings: A Narrative of Trees* (London: Chatto & Windus, 2007), p. ix. BBC news ran a story on 15 October 2012 entitled, '25 Years On: How Great Storm Permanently Changed Landscape', including eyewitness testimony: www.bbc.co.uk/news/uk-19947449 (accessed 19 October 2012).

17 Peter Goodwin, 'Mulberry Burr versus Stained Burr Maple', *Woodland Heritage* (2006), pp. 38–39 (p. 38).

18 Titchmarsh & Goodwin archive.

19 Edward H. Pinto, 'The Myth of the Mulberry Burr Veneer', *Country Life*, 2 October 1969, pp. 794–795 (p. 794).

20 Goodwin, 'Mulberry Burr', p. 13.

21 Percy Macquoid and Ralph Edwards, *The Dictionary of English Furniture*, 3 vols (Woodbridge: The Antique Collectors' Club, 1983 [1954]), vol. 1, p. 138.

22 Heal, *The London Furniture Makers*, Figures 12 and 13 (pp. 230–231).

23 Advertisement in *Country Life*, 9 June 1988, p. 153.

24 See www.britishmuseum.org/research/collection_online/collection_object_details.aspx?objectId=55446&partId=1&searchText=Mulberry+Tompion+clock&page=1.

25 Bowett, *English Furniture, 1660–1714*, pp. 224–226.

26 Adam Bowett, *Early Georgian Furniture, 1715–1740*

(Woodbridge: The Antique Collectors' Club, 2009).

27 Adam Bowett, 'Stained Burr Maple v. Burr Mulberry' (with a short reply by Peter Goodwin), *Woodland Heritage* (2008), pp. 62–63.

28 Adam Bowett, 'Furniture Woods in London and Provincial Furniture, 1700–1800', *Regional Furniture Journal*, 22 (2008), pp. 87–113 (p. 92).

29 Bowett, 'Stained Burr Maple', p. 63.

30 Furniture catalogue, *Fine English Furniture including the Georgian and Regency Period* (2012) produced by Titchmarsh & Goodwin. The illustration is on p. 75.

31 Stephen Bowe, 'A Rare Japanese Mulberry Wood Called Shimakuwa', *Woodland Heritage* (2009), pp. 24–25.

32 Kazuko Koizumi, *Traditional Japanese Furniture: A Definitive Guide*, translated by Alfred Birnbaum (Tokyo: Kodansha International, 1986). Some sixteenth-century informal ornamental shelves, kazari-dana, are shown on p. 40 and twentieth-century pieces, including a full-length mirror, on p. 66.

33 *Japanese Crafts: A Complete Guide to Today's Traditional Handmade Objects*, with an introduction by Diane Durston (Tokyo: Kodansha International, 1996), p. 124, and also a beautiful illustration on p. 125.

34 Felice Fischer (ed.), *The Art of Japanese Craft: 1875 to Present* (New Haven, Conn.: Philadelphia Museum of Art, in association with Yale University Press, 2008), p. 43. This was produced as part of an exhibition at the Philadelphia Museum of Art which ran from December 2008 to autumn 2009.

35 Gian Carlo Calza, *Japan Style* (London: Phaidon Press, 2007). 'Tea Time in Japan circa 1900' appears in the chapter 'Irregular Beauty' (p. 26).

36 Marie-France Boyer, 'Japan in Soft Focus', *World of Interiors*, 31.6 (2011), pp. 136–145, with specific reference to the photograph by Albert Kahn (p. 139).

37 Koizumi, *Traditional Japanese Furniture*, p. 184.

38 See 'Sashimono Furniture', in the NHK World television series, *Begin Japanology*, presented by Peter Barakan and first broadcast in Japan in 2011.

39 See Jesse Russell and Ronald Cohn, *Izu Islands* (Edinburgh: Bookvika Publishing, 2012).

40 Jun Saito, *Tokyo no shima* [Islands of Tokyo] (Tokyo: Kobunsha, 2007). Translated for this publication by Minako Jackson in 2012.

41 Koizumi, *Traditional Japanese Furniture*, p. 184.

42 Tsukada Kyoko, 'We Have Nurtured Trees since Time Immemorial to Get the Precious Drops', *Kateigaho International*, winter edition (2007), p. 39.

43 See n. 38, above.

44 Koizumi, *Traditional Japanese Furniture*. Joinery is featured on pp. 185–194, with a number of illustrations.

45 Elizabeth Kiritani, *Vanishing Japan: Traditions, Crafts and Culture* (Tokyo: Tuttle Publishing, 1995), p. 84.

46 *A History of the World in 100 Objects*, BBC Radio 4 series, written and presented by Neil MacGregor, first broadcast January–October 2010, www.bbc.co.uk/podcasts/series/ahow. The series was a partnership between Radio 4 and the British Museum. Repackaged in a 20 CD box set, with illustrated booklet (AudioGo Ltd., 2011). See also, *A History of the World in 100 Objects* (London: Allen Lane, 2010)

47 Saito, *Tokyo no shima*.

48 See Nicole Rousmaniere (ed.), *Crafting Beauty in Modern Japan* (London: British Museum Press, 2007). This was produced to accompany an exhibition which ran from July to October 2007. See item Number 96 (p. 131).

49 Rupert Faulkner, *Japanese Studio Crafts Tradition and the Avant-Garde* (London: Laurence King, 1995), Plate 42.

50 Kiritani, *Vanishing Japan*, p. 87.

51 See www.edocraft.com (accessed 1 October 2012).

52 See Takaaki Nishikawa, *Nihon no mori to ki no Shokunin* [Forests in Japan and Craftsmen of Wood] (Tokyo: Diamond Big Co., 2007). Translated for this publication by Angela Davies in 2008.

53 www.earthquake.usgs.gov (accessed 22 October 2012).

54 In private correspondence dated 2 September 2007 to the author from Mr Sugiyama of Kichizo.

55 *Distinguished Designs including the Dunhill Collection of Namiki Pens*, catalogue for a sale held at Bonhams, London, 30 November 2011.

56 Nick Foulkes and Charles March, *Dunhill by Design: A Very English Story* (Paris: Flammarion, 2006), pp. 124–126.

57 *You Only Live Twice*, Lewis Gilbert (dir.), 'Ultimate 007 Edition', Metro Goldwyn Mayer (1967). Produced in DVD format for MGM Home Entertainment.

58 Bowe, 'A Rare Japanese Mulberry Wood'.

59 Graves, *Seeing Things Differently*. The quotation is taken from the section 'Maker and Marketplace' (p. 42).

60 'Chuck Out Your Chintz', television advertising campaign for IKEA in the United Kingdom (1996).

61 Kerry Capell, 'Ikea's New Plan for Japan', *Business Week*, 25 April 2006: www.bloomberg.com/bw/stories/2006-04-25/ikeas-new-plan-for-japan (accessed 12 September 2012).

63 Japanese ceramic
thick tea container with
mulberry wood lid

4

Ritual and Custom

Introduction

This chapter will in the main focus on the craft tradition in Japan, comparing the objects with some of those items produced for and found in contemporary United Kingdom markets. In addition, the ritual of the tea ceremony will be discussed in relation to mulberry wood and particularly shimakuwa mulberry. Finally, the Mingei and Kokten Korgei traditions will be reviewed in relation to two exhibitions. The first was a travelling exhibition organised by the Mingei International Museum of World Folk Art in 1995 and the second took place at Blackwell, The Arts and Crafts House, in Bowness-on-Windermere, Cumbria, in 2001.

Japan has the richest variety of mulberry wood items in the world and this is particularly true of small objects. This includes not only objects with mulberry-related imagery as decoration on the surface but also those made of mulberry wood and particularly associated with the tea ceremony. A very high proportion of items are crafted rather than mass-produced and the tradition of craft, Mingei and Kokten Korgei, will be briefly discussed later. Japan is a culture which values skill and clearly its long craft tradition is one based around the maker, aesthetics, ritual and custom. A significant factor in much of the craft is that it is not dependent on time constraints; for example, the application of lacquer is very time consuming and weaving by hand requires patience. The objects featured in this chapter indicate their value to the users but also the qualities they value. In the book *Japanese Crafts* we read: 'Cutting corners is not part of the Japanese craftsman's vocabulary. The real evidence of their ingenuity and meticulous workmanship is hidden beneath the silent layers of immaculately finished surface.'[1]

Japan has a network of galleries and museums to exhibit and promote craft; for example, the National Museums of Modern Art, in Tokyo and Kyoto, which have in their collections various objects ranging from ceramics to textiles, lacquer, wood and bamboo. For a significant period, the Japanese government has endeavoured to promote craft and there are craft centres within the Tokyo area, including the Japan Traditional Craft Centre located in the Metropolitan Plaza Building. Products are allowed to be exhibited if they fulfil certain criteria as specified by the Minister of Economy, Trade and Industry, which are as follows:

1. The article must be used mainly in everyday life.

2. The article must be primarily manufactured by hand.

3. The article must be manufactured using traditional techniques having a history of at least 100 years.

4. The main materials used in their making are those which have been used traditionally.

5. The industry must be of a regional nature.

The Centre issues a certificate of authenticity for each of the craft items it sells and also promotes its activities abroad via exhibitions and public relations events. Japan still retains a regional focus for particular objects and this is reviewed below. By way of contrast, examples of UK-based work are also featured when appropriate.

Ceramics and Silk

The regional focus of craft work is reviewed in *Japanese Crafts*,[2] which was produced in cooperation with the Japan craft forum. Again, crafts are described and organised by material, with chapters on ceramics, textiles, lacquer ware, bamboo craft, Japanese paper, woodcraft, metalwork and specific crafts such as Gifu lanterns. In a number of cases there is a connection with mulberry wood or else the products are processed directly or indirectly from the *Morus alba* tree. All of the materials are traditional and the objects are handmade using long-established skills and techniques. The first example is Bizen ware (Illustration 63). This ceramic comes from the oldest established kilns in Japan. The unglazed stoneware is unusual because many of the effects on the surface are reliant on chance and are the result of the firing techniques used on the clay. The Bizen potters introduced new kilns in the nineteenth century and started to create drinking vessels and tea ceremony items. The chaire (green tea container) shown in Illustration 63 has a Bizen base with the addition of a turned and stained mulberry wood lid. The decoration is based on a hidasuki method, which involves winding straw around the leather-hard ceramic and firing it at a relatively high temperature – this leaves a red 'ghost' mark on the surface. In the United Kingdom, Svend Bayer – who has travelled to Japan to view their wood-fired kilns and importantly was a pupil of Michael Cardew – produces similar but larger-scale work.[3] Bizen ceramics can be classed as part of the Mingei tradition and this will be discussed later in this chapter.

The Bizen chaire featured has an associated ikat silk shifuku (shown in the tea cabinet in Illustration 33) and the knotting has to be done in a precise way; YouTube has lessons on how to do it. Ikat textiles are very common in Japan and are featured in the book *Japanese Ikat* as part of the Kyoto Shoin's Art Library of Japanese Textiles.[4] The genre can be divided by material type, including cotton, ramie and silk. The silk textiles produced in Japan have a particularly rich tradition and there are numerous examples

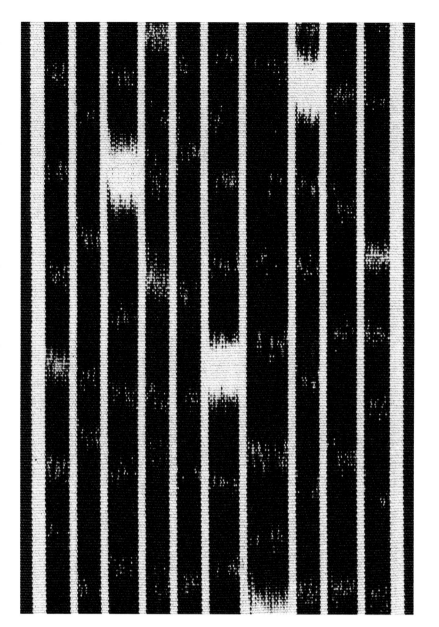

64 English hand woven monochrome silk ikat fabric, by Mary Restieaux

of kasuri/ikat fabrics, including those produced at Isesaki, Gunma prefecture. The Isesaki kasuri is a silk cloth that was first produced around the sixteenth century and was generally woven from leftover silk and tamamayu in a resist method using both the warp and weft threads. A description of the process is featured in Nicole Rousmaniere's *Crafting Beauty in Modern Japan*.[5] There are contemporary Japanese makers such as Imai Yoko, who weaves in silk using a warp and weft kasuri. This is shown on the front cover of *The Japanese Craft Tradition*.[6] In the United Kingdom, a contemporary weaver using only warp resist ikat is Mary Restieaux (Illustration 64). She is a renowned craftsperson working solely in silk using the ikat process. She received a traditional craft award in Kyoto in 1994 and was made a fellow of the Royal College of Art in 1995. Her work has been extensively exhibited and a summary of her activity is featured in the catalogue *Age of Experience*.[7] Her work has also been reviewed in the journal *Crafts* and is much admired abroad, being in the collections of the National Museum of Modern Art in Kyoto.[8] From 1991, she has also designed under the First Eleven Studio banner, including a silk fabric called Monsoon Wedding for the Italian textile producer Rubelli. Both Mary Restieaux and Isesaki ikat have the characteristic feathering of the pattern, although in the case of the Isesaki kasuri the ikat patterns locate both vertically and horizontally while in those produced by Mary Restieaux the patterns fall vertically along the woven fabric.

In addition to these silk ikats another noteworthy silk fabric is produced on one of the Izu islands, Hachijojima. The silk tsumugi is famous for its extremely bright yellow (similar to the spider silk fabric featured in Chapter 1), which is called ki and has been produced on the islands for over 500 years. The yellow colour is achieved by a natural dye sourced from a grass grown on the island. Unusually, the island's name comes from the silk fabric and relates to its production length of 3 metres – in Japanese this is called hachi-jo. In their book *Izu Islands* Jesse Russell and Ronald Cohn write that Hachijojima is a compound low-activity volcanic island with both a caldera and some pyroclastic cones.[9] The main activity on the island now is tourism and one of the silk textile producing workshops is open to the public.

Wood and Lacquer

The wood or furniture tradition in Japan is discussed in Chapter 3, but there are also examples of woodwork that use mulberry wood alongside many other woods such as Hakone marquetry. This highly decorative work combines various woods of different colours including cream, black, brown, red and yellow (mulberry). Wood workers in the area of Yumoto are surrounded by the mountains and forests of Hakone which have a rich diversity of tree species to use in their work. Fundamentally, the process is based on adhering different woods together in various patterns (there are many hundreds, from the simple to the complex) and creating veneers which can be applied to wooden items for decorative effect – this has been called wooden patchwork. The work is remarkably similar to the wooden items called Tunbridge Ware that were produced in the United Kingdom in the eighteenth and nineteenth centuries, including tessellated mosaics composed of different coloured woods, including mulberry.[10] There is an extensive collection in the Tunbridge Wells Museum and Art Gallery[11] and numerous antique dealers specialise in the ware, which can range from furniture items to small novelties and holiday mementos (Illustration 65). In Japan solid wood banded pieces can sometimes be created and this is seen in tea ceremony ware, including natsume and kogo. David Linley, the UK-based handmade furniture company that specialises in marquetry (see the humidors in their gifts and

65 Japanese Hakone wood thin green tea container and English Tunbridge Ware snuff box (middle)

accessories catalogue),[12] has sold solid Hakone turned wooden items under its own brand (Illustration 65) and also veneered Hakone secret boxes (called marquetry tricks boxes) on its website.[13]

Japanese artisans have also developed lacquer ware to a very high degree of sophistication, such as that found in Wakayama prefecture. In the main the core for the application of lacquer is wood and this is the case with the natsume as featured in Illustration 66. This object is turned in wood and incised decoration in the form of vertical ribs is applied, intended to make the green tea caddy look like a pumpkin. This then has a series of layers of dark red lacquer applied so that it pools within the ridges. Interestingly, in these examples the lid is stained and turned mulberry wood. There are also Japanese examples of sculptural tea caddies such as those made into gourd shapes (Illustration 67).

In the United Kingdom, there is a tradition of having tea caddies shaped in the form of fruits such as apples and pears (Illustration 68). Occasionally, there are also some vegetable shapes found such as pumpkins and aubergines. In the main these were produced during the Georgian period when there was a fashion for

tea consumption, and because tea was expensive the caddies were used for safe storage – they nearly always had a lock and key. Victor H. Mair and Erling Hoh's *The True History of Tea* indicates that tea was priced between £6 and £10 per lb (450 gm) in 1650 – equivalent to £500 and £800 in today's money.[14] It would appear that tea remained exorbitantly priced late into the eighteenth century. The English East India Company proved critical in the tea trade as well as introducing ceramics from Jingdezhen into the country. Tea has become connected with the drinking habits of the United Kingdom and since the opening of the first tea house in 1717 by Thomas Twining and the Vauxhall tea gardens in 1732 it has established itself as a favourite beverage for both men and women. The walnut caddy featured in Illustration 68 is later in date and was produced during the late Victorian period. Tea at that time was more abundant and readily available which meant that there was no need for security. In addition to powdered green tea storage in the form of natsume and chaire the Japanese also use caddies for storing black and green leaf tea, and an example made of mulberry wood can be seen in Illustration 69.

66 Japanese lacquer thin green tea container with mulberry wood lid

67 Japanese mulberry wood thin green tea container

68 English Victorian
walnut wood leaf tea
caddy (apple form)

69 Japanese mulberry
wood leaf tea container

Bamboo and Paper

Bamboo grows throughout Japan in both natural and man-made contexts. It is a natural resource and is used extensively in a variety of traditional and contemporary crafts. One supreme example is the Takayama tea whisks made in Ikoma, Nara prefecture. These chasen are also made in Kyoto and Nagoya but those produced in Ikoma constitute the majority of those in circulation in Japan. The whisk is made of split bamboo (Illustration 70) and can be found in a number of different types depending on the bamboo and also the number of splines or spines. The whisks or chasen have a number of splines which are arranged into an inner (uchiho) and outer ring (sotoho) in a ratio of 4:6. They are kept in place with a silk or cotton thread and the splines are carved, curled and arranged accordingly. It is clearly an object of simple beauty and in addition it also has functionality – it whisks the green tea into the water and because it is soft also protects the precious tea bowl. In *Japanese Crafts* it states: 'The chasen illustrates well the dilemma that a fine object of Japanese craftwork often presents – whether to use it, or just admire it as a work of art.'[15] Along with the chasen there is also an associated rest (Illustration 71) called a chasen kusenaoshi, which is used to straighten and dry the whisk after it is used in the tea ceremony. The examples featured are made of mulberry wood.

Along with *Morus alba* as a source of mulberry wood there is also a mulberry paper tree (*Broussonetia papyrifera*) that is grown in Japan specifically for the manufacture of washi papers. Awa washi is produced in Yamakawa-cho, Tokushima prefecture, and has been manufactured in the region for over 1,000 years. The raw materials used for Awa washi include kozo, mitsumata and ganpi. The paper-making sieve screens are made out of bamboo and these are used in the nagashisuki method of paper making. A speciality of the process can sometimes be the inclusion of an indigo dye which turns the paper a distinctive denim blue colour. Since the late 1700s, the Fujimori family has carried on the tradition of Awa washi and they are still manufacturing into the twenty-first century. In 1976, Awa washi was designated as an Intangible Cultural Property of Tokushima prefecture and Minoru Fujimori was selected as a master craftsman. Techniques were later passed on to Yoichi Fujimori and he has also introduced machine-made washi paper which can now be purchased worldwide under the Awagami Factory brand.[16]

Alongside paper for calligraphy and painting,

mulberry paper can also be used to craft objects and an example of this is the manufacture of lanterns, which combines paper and bamboo. These are made at Gifu in the Gifu prefecture and for many people these lights are intrinsically associated with Eastern culture and Japan in particular. They come in various shapes, including spheres, cylinders and a natsumegata form that is based on the natsume used in the tea ceremony. The lights can be decorated with naturalistic imagery and have a variety of different decorative and functional stands depending on which room they are to be placed in. Isamu Noguchi (1904–1988) was an artist, sculptor and designer, of American Japanese extraction. His life and work have featured in the *Modern Masters* series.[17] Noguchi was instrumental in

70 Japanese mulberry wood whisk shaper with bamboo tea whisk

71 Japanese mulberry
wood tea whisk shapers

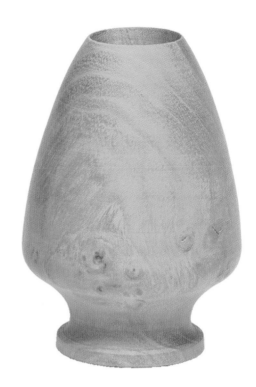

designing the Akari light in the Gifu region of Japan (see Illustration 72). It is recorded that in 1951 Noguchi visited the Nagara River to observe the famous cormorant fishing, and while there he made drawings of the illumination on the fishing boats. He was interested in the elegance and simplicity of the light shade and had an idea to create new markets by combining modern design with traditional craft techniques. He followed the traditional shapes as a guide and modified the structure for the electric light bulb. In the Vitra catalogue for Isamu Noguchi Akari lights it states:

> The fabrication of Akari Light Sculptures in Japan at Ozeki and Co. Ltd., since 1952 follows the traditional methods for Japanese Gifu lanterns. Each Akari Light Sculpture is hand crafted beginning with the making of Shoji paper from the inner bark of the mulberry tree. Bamboo ribbing is stretched across wooden molded forms which resemble sculpture. The Shoji paper is cut into wide or narrow strips depending upon the size and shape of the lamp and then glued onto both sides of the framework. Once the glue has dried and the shape is set, the internal wooden form is disassembled and removed.

> The outcome is a resilient paper form which can be collapsed and packed flat for shipping.[18]

Eventually, dozens of different shapes were created mainly in plain white paper for the export market and these were retailed across the world. In fact, in the *Modern Masters* book it states that over 100 models are still manufactured at Gifu[19] and some are available to purchase via the furniture retailers/manufacturers Vitra.[20]

Mulberry Imagery on Historic Items

Japan is a major producer of silk, and sericulture imagery can be found in various Japanese objects. A late nineteenth-century tobacco pouch, now in the collection of the Boston Museum of Fine Arts, moves from two-dimensional imagery of mulberry leaves on a silk textile background to additional three-dimensional attached objects. These include a pouch with an image of a half-eaten mulberry leaf painted in gold on the silk by Teikwa and carved ivory silk moths and a worm crafted by Kwaigyokusai Masatsugu. In addition, there is an ojime, which is a carved, maroon-stained wooden mulberry fruit with a green ivory stalk and a netsuke in carved unstained ivory in the form of a silk cocoon. Thus, the object encompasses the entire life cycle of *Bombyx mori* in all its forms, and these objects are attached to a purse made out of the resultant material (blue brocaded silk). It is probably the best object related to sericulture in the world. A description in *The Art Bulletin* states:

> Our pouch and its ornaments take us through some of the processes of the growth of the silkworm. First, on the back of the pouch, a skilfully carved larva, fastened to the cloth, is realistically eating a mulberry leaf, painted in gold. After three rests and a great deal of feeding in between, the silkworms take their 'great rest', and spin a silk cocoon. The netsuke represents such a cocoon; the ivory is about the same creamy white as the real cocoon and is carved to represent its rough surface and the characteristic indentation in the centre. When the moths emerge from the cocoons, they soon pair; and the clasp on our pouch skilfully represents this process, the female moth on one side being made larger than the male on the other side, as is really the case. The ojime, made of wood stained purple or maroon, with a green ivory stem, looks just like a mulberry fruit, and the cord passes through a half-eaten leaf, made of *kiri* (pawlonia) wood, on top of the pouch. The elaborate affair in all probability adorned the person of some young dandy.[21]

A similar European object featuring a mulberry fruit is in the collections of the British Museum as part of the Hull Grundy gift (Museum Number 1978-1002.930.a) and comprises a brooch made of coloured gold and dark purple amethyst in the form of a mulberry fruit, branch and leaves in a naturalistic arrangement. The brooch was made around 1850 and has the addition of an enamelled red ladybird on one of the leaves. The ladybird is associated with luck and the heart-shaped leaves of the mulberry are associated with love. The purple amethyst is symbolic of sincerity – so the brooch could have been gifted with sincere love and attached luck. Another Japanese object with sericulture imagery is a superb inro in the collections of the V&A (Museum Number W307-1922). The inro is essentially a container worn with the kimono because it had no pockets and was used to store small items such as a seal and ink. It dates from 1865 and was made by a master Shibata Zeshin (1807–1891). It is a tiered container fixed by a knotted cord, decorated using complex lacquer techniques and it encompasses abstract images of mulberry leaves, silk moths and cocoons. It is part of a set of 12 depicting the calendar months and is a tour de force of lacquer craft.

Zeshin's work is featured in Raymond Bushell's *Inro Handbook*, including an inro with decoration of birds in flight over a silvery moon made of mulberry wood with the grain showing as part of the background.[22] The inro has a round coral ojime and a lacquer netsuke. In Japan imagery usually has symbolic significance, like the European brooch, and the leaves of the mulberry are used as receptacles for food offerings to the Shinto gods. The Japanese also associate the mulberry with the Weaver Girl in the Tanabata Festival (observed on the seventh day of the seventh month) and they often place strips of mulberry paper on to sacred trees. It is sometimes very difficult exactly to identify specific woods in netsuke and this is discussed by Julia Hutt in her book *Japanese Netsuke*. Various netsuke were photographed for the publication with fruit and vegetables such as bean pods, persimmon and pumpkin.[23] Occasionally, imagery associated with the mulberry tree can be found but it is rare – a wood netsuke entitled *Quail under a Mulberry Branch* was for sale in 2007. Imagery featuring sericulture including silkworms and mulberry leaves is also evident in a superb ivory ojime attributed to Kaigyokusai Masatsugu.[24]

Japan has some of the oldest recorded crafted ceramics, with some dating from 5000 BC. Neil MacGregor describes one Jomon pot in his *A History of the World in 100 Objects*:

> Nowadays Jomon pots are used as cultural ambassadors for Japan in major exhibitions around the world. Most nations, when presenting themselves abroad, look back to imperial glories or invading armies. Remarkably, technological, economically powerful Japan proudly proclaims its identity in the creations of the early hunter-gathers ... for the Jomon's meticulous attention to detail and patterning, the search for ever-greater aesthetic refinement and the long continuity of Jomon traditions seem already very Japanese.[25]

The simple Jomon pot has even more to give with regard to its history because when it was discovered the interior surfaces were lined with gold by a collector. It then became a precious tea ceremony artefact called a mizusashi or water jar – the functionality valued alongside its tradition. The tea ceremony and the objects used within it are quintessentially Japanese and many of the items have been created in mulberry and particularly shimakuwa.

Tea Ceremony – Chanoyu and Temae – Process and Variation

Tea houses and sites for the tea ceremony can be found throughout Japan, with some found in Tokyo, Osaka, Kanazawa, Matsue and Inuyama, but a good proportion are located in the cultural capital at Kyoto.[26] Many are open to view and can have the most beautiful attached gardens

72 Japanese mulberry paper Akari light shade, by Isamu Noguchi

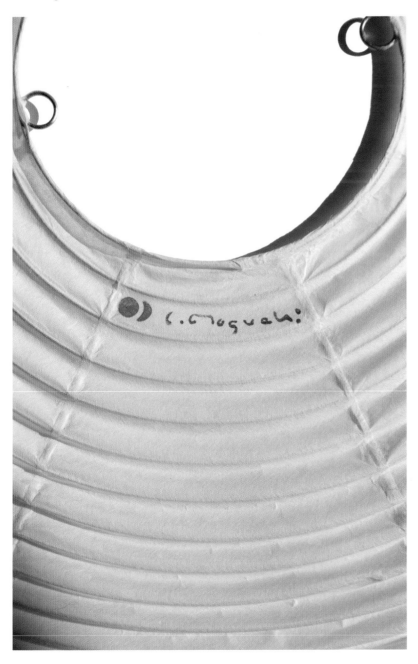

such as the one at Dai Nihon Chado Gakkai. The aesthetic of the architecture of the tea room has been much documented and has even featured in a 2005 advertising campaign for the retail company MUJI (Mujirushi Ryohin). Contemporary developments have featured tree tea houses and some of these have been photographed in Sadako Ohki's *Tea Culture of Japan*.[27] Renowned architects such as Tadao Ando have designed tea rooms and the British Museum has recreated a tea room in its Mitsubishi galleries. Contemporary designers have also used the ceremony for inspiration, including a tea cabinet or chadansu by the American maker Douglas Brooks of Vermont. The catalogue for the *Shaker Design: Out of this World* exhibition in 2008 states:

> Although the Shaker and Japanese furniture making traditions developed independently on opposite sides of the world, they share a common design philosophy that emphasizes simplicity, honesty, and utility. Both traditions incorporate the concept that form follows function, an idea that is reflected in the asymmetry of their respective case furniture.[28]

In the book *Japan Style* it states: 'Foremost among the concepts that Asia has passed to the West are those connected with the world of tea – a short word with a vast and complex range of associations.'[29] It is clear that theories and debates associated with the tea ceremony have become overcomplicated, though if you look at the objects the actual process is remarkably simple – nearly as easy as placing a tea bag into a cup. It is the crafting and making of the objects that is sophisticated and refined. In a book which accompanied an exhibition relating to the tea culture in Japan, Sadako Ohki writes about chanoyu, which means 'hot water for tea':

> The practice of chanoyu is a dynamic and multidimensional activity that encompasses many art forms and all the human senses. If you experience a small intimate tea gathering as a guest, the cares of the world will start to lift as soon as you walk on the moist stepping stones of the garden, sit at a covered waiting bench (machiai), and rinse your hands and mouth at a water basin (tsukubai). After you discard social hierarchy by

lowering your head to enter the tea room on your knees, as do all the guests, you will feel the texture of the tatami mat, admire in the tokonoma alcove a hanging scroll selected for you, inhale a whiff of subtle incense, taste a simple but elegant meal from the mountain and sea, and listen to the sound of steam – likened to wind through pine trees – rising from a small opening in the knob of an iron kettle lid. The host of the gathering takes the lid off the kettle, sets it down on the lid rest, and scoops out boiling water that is poured into a tea bowl with powdered green tea, which is then whipped with a bamboo whisk. You observe these carefully choreographed gestures of the host, share in the bowing and the handling of the tea-filled bowl, and finally taste the bitter whipped green tea after finishing a sweet confection.[30]

The tea ceremony has a very long history, which is reviewed in *The True History of Tea*.[31]

Japan features in two separate chapters dealing first with developments from the twelfth to the fifteenth centuries and secondly what is termed the perfection of the tea ceremony. A tea chronology can be found in *The Tea Ceremony*.[32] It is not within the scope of this present work to delve into the history of the ceremony because in the main it is the ceremony itself and the objects used within it that are important for this study. Needless to say, it is a complex subject area in both its history and the technicalities of the process in its many variations. In *The True History of Tea* we read:

> In the chanoyu established by Rikyu and practised with variations to this day, there is a difference between the winter ceremony, known as Ro, in which the hearth (ro) is positioned in a space cut out in the middle of the room, and the summer ceremony, called Furo, where a portable brazier (furo) is positioned in a corner of the room to reduce the discomfort from the heat, and placed on a tray, board, or special type of square tile to protect the straw mat.[33]

There is both a formal and an informal tea ceremony and each component within these ceremonies can be adjusted slightly from day to day and season to season. A guide to how to perform a simple tea ceremony is detailed in *The Book of Tea*.[34] While the technicalities feature over 1,000 variations (temae) in the making of tea – virtually every nuance of movement is dictated and has a purpose – formality, manners and sequence are critical aspects of the process. There are three basic elements associated with temae and they are arrangement, purification and calmness of mind. The arrangement of the various items within the context or the room is important for the smooth operation of the ceremony and it is the decision of the tea master as to what spatial arrangement he uses. The objects arranged near to the master are those that are central to the actual making of the tea and include the tea caddy (either a natsume or chaire), scoop or chasaku, whisk or chasen and the tea bowl. The ceremony and to a degree the objects are dictated by whether the ceremony is for thick or thin tea. For example, a natsume is used for thin tea and a chaire is used for thick tea. The powdered green tea (usucha) is exactly the same in both cases but the proportion of powder to hot water differs. The purification is featured in *The Tea Ceremony* where it states:

> The cleaning of the tea container and the tea scoop (chashaku) is an important act, for it signi-fies a spiritual cleansing of the mind and heart, during which all thoughts pertaining to the tem-poral world should be dismissed. When making koicha or thick tea, the ceramic tea container is wiped first with a folded silk cloth called a fukusa. Similarly in the preparation of usucha, thin tea, it is the lacquered tea container that is wiped first.[35]

The tranquillity of the process is achieved by the environment being very controlled and calm. This is aided by the tea house often having an attached garden which brings the partici-pant closer to nature and the actual process. A beautiful garden as part of a tea room built by Sen Sotan at Kyoto (Urasenke) was featured as Garden 45 in Monty Don's *Around the World in 80 Gardens*[36] and there is also a good exam-ple in the United Kingdom at Tatton Park, in Cheshire, which celebrated the Japanese gar-den's centenary in 2010. The garden includes a Shinto shrine and small tea house and is prob-ably one of the best examples in Europe. An article in *Homes & Gardens* features some of the best general examples – Kenroku-en, Koraku-en and Kairaku-en.[37] Virtually every aspect of the tea ceremony has variations, which mean that the processes are extremely difficult to describe succinctly. However, the aspects that remain relatively fixed are the objects associated with the ceremony, including items made from fabric, ceramic, metal, bamboo and, impor-tantly, wood.

Tea Ceremony – Object and Artefact

Fundamental to the tea ceremony are the objects which are used for storage or as tools in the drinking, preparation and enjoyment of tea. In Morgan Pitelka's *Japanese Tea Culture*, a case study of a contemporary tea ceremony records and details all the utensils used for the tea gathering, and includes a total of 22 items.[38] The gathering was held at the Tsuki-no-Ma hall at the Iwaka Shrine, Western Tokyo, and was hosted by Konno Soen on 14 March 1993. The objects and particularly the bowl (Illustration 16) play a very important part in the symbolic nature of the tea ceremony. This is because it comes into direct contact with both the host and the guests. There are over 40 items associ-ated with the tea ceremony and many of them are wooden. These include very small items such as the tea scoop or chasaku (Illustration 62) as well as substantial tea shelves or cha dansu (Illustration 33), which are used to store all the items. The ceremony is very contemplative and encompasses all of the senses including smell (small ceramic or wooden vessels called kogo, for example, are used to hold incense) (Illustration 61). In addition, the items are intended to be visually stimulating on every level and often the highest-quality objects are used for the process, including shimakuwa items. These are often hand crafted and consid-erable care is taken in their placement within the room and also their location within the tea ceremony cabinet. The various larger items for the tea ceremony are shown in Illustration 33 and have attached numbers which will be cited in the text. Virtually all the objects featured in this photograph are made out of mulberry wood. Some of the wood has been stained, some has a limed finish and other pieces have a fancy or moiré grain which tends to be in the natu-ral colour. The largest item is the tea cabinet (Illustration 33, labelled 3), produced *c.*1925, which is used to house smaller tea ceremony items; here it contains on the offset shelves in the glazed area a ikat silk shifuko and ceram-ics including a vase for flower arrangements (for example, in the alcove of the tea room – cha-bana) and two tea bowls.

Flower arranging, like so many aspects of the tea ceremony, paradoxically, can be simple but also very complicated. It appears that arrangements should reflect the seasons and be more informal than the ikebana style. Often it can just be a single bloom but this must be able to be viewed and admired by the guests. All the ceramic items in the tea cabinet have the impressed mark CAR, and are made in porcelain with a black crackle glaze finish. CAR stands for Christine Ann Richards, a craftsperson based in the United Kingdom who has travelled extensively to the Far East including both China and Japan (Tokomane) to study glazes and production. Her work is influenced by the oriental aesthetic and a selection of her porcelain pieces can be used in the tea ceremony.[39] There is also a pine box with yellow ribbon intended to house a tea scoop and this is placed on the right-hand side on the lower shelf in the glazed area. The cabinet is made from a case of zelkova and paulownia with the front featuring hinged/sliding doors and drawers veneered with mulberry wood that has a very fancy moiré grain. On top of the cabinet are two items not directly associated with the ceremony. The first is a twentieth-century five-compartment writing box (suzuri-bako) in limed mulberry similar to that featured in the book *Traditional Japanese Furniture*, which is a seventeenth-century example.[40] The compartments contain an ink stone, ink block, water container and a bamboo brush used for calligraphy. The second item is a sewing box or hari-bako, which again is produced using similar woods to the tea cabinet, and this piece is a smaller version of the one featured in Illustration 41 with the convoluted grain being clearly seen on the front. Both sewing cabinets date from the middle of the twentieth century, though this furniture form is no longer used in contemporary Japan. Clothes tend to be discarded rather than repaired by the younger generation and in most cases traditional furniture forms have been replaced by westernised contemporary examples, such as television stands.

Other furniture featured includes a portable shelving system (Illustration 33, labelled 4) in stained mulberry (mid-twentieth century). This is collapsible and can be carried by the tea master – in the photograph it displays two peach bloom porcelain pieces (suitable for a kogo and mizusashi) by CAR. The movable mulberry screen produced in the mid-twentieth century (Illustration 33, labelled 5) is used to

74 Japanese mulberry wood thin green tea container

display textiles or to block the view of items from tea ceremony guests when needed. In this case a fabric called Flint, handmade of cotton/silk with ikat pattern, is featured which was produced in Japan for the Naga Collection by Andrew Martin, an interior design company based in the United Kingdom. Further items featured in this montage include a stained mulberry wood brazier (Illustration 33, labelled 6) with metal cast iron kettle and a stained mulberry tray (Illustration 33, labelled 7) with mulberry natsume and mulberry handled metal chopsticks (for handling heated charcoal). All the furniture is placed on a tatami mat with dimensions of 90 cm × 180 cm. This is the common flooring material within the tea room and various room types can be classified by the number of mats on the floor.

Mulberry wood is a very common material for making tea ceremony items and features in numerous examples, from the relatively inexpensive to the very expensive, as is the case with shimakuwa or island mulberry pieces. Many of the inexpensive pieces, whilst being handmade, are produced in large numbers and tend not to have any associated packaging or maker's mark. None of the items featured in Illustration 33 has been directly signed and makers can only be identified via the packaging or box. While tea utensils are permanently stored in tea cabinets, if the tea master has to move to different locations it is often the case that he will carry the essential items in a box called a chabako. A selection of these have been illustrated (Illustrations 37 and 39) and show the different mulberry woods. The interior of the box has an upper dividing tray (as shown in Illustration 37). This is intended to store the tea scoop (often made of bamboo) and textile items such as the cleaning cloths and a silk wallet that houses small items such as sweet papers and a fan. In addition, it can also contain a cloth for the arrangement of items such as the one illustrated in Illustration 73. The items stored in the bottom of the box include those featured in Illustration 40 and comprise a kogo for incense, natsume for green tea powder and the tea whisk (chasen) contained within a turned protective wooden case called a kusenaoshi. These items can match but sometimes it is considered that the items are best mismatched. The boxes associated with tea utensil storage have featured in many exhibitions, including the British Museum's 2007 *Crafting Beauty in Modern Japan*, which featured a sand-polished Japanese larch box for utensils made for tea gatherings created in 1964 by Himi Kodo (1906–1975).[41] He was designated a national living treasure in 1970 for his wood craft (moku kogei) techniques.

75 Japanese mulberry wood thin green tea container

Tea Caddy – Natsume and Chaire

There is a basic subdivision of powdered green tea (usucha) containers into those used for thin tea, the natsume, and those intended for use with thick tea, the chaire. Often they come packaged in boxes that can be made of paulownia or pine and the better quality ones are also signed. In the case of tea containers they can also have an accompanying shifoku or silk bag which is used for protection and decoration, the corded silk bag being more common in chaire than natsume. The chaires are nearly always made of ceramic of various types and often have turned ivory lids with small knob handles. In certain examples the chaire can have a turned mulberry wood lid, as is the case in Illustration 63, and this item also has a tight inner lid, which keeps the tea fresh. There are complete books in Japanese that simply catalogue and describe various chaires alongside their considerable history and usage. Chaires that have associations with specific tea masters are revered and can reach premium prices; one shown in Seno Tanaka and Sendo Tanaka's *The Tea Ceremony* features a Chinese-made ceramic owned by Sen no Rikyu that has no fewer than four attached shifuku for its display and protection.[42] Sen no Rikyu created a wabi style ceremony which forms the basis of many of the tea ceremonies which take place today. He lived from 1522 to 1591 and his work is featured in most of the books related to tea in Japan. Generally, both chaires and natsume are of a similar size and can be readily held in the hand. Green tea (Ryokucha) does not have a long life and can deteriorate over a short time frame, so the containers only really have enough powdered tea for a few ceremonies.

The natsume tea caddy is a very rich source for study because there are so many different types in terms of the shape (they are nearly always turned wood) and also the material, featuring various woods (over 30 identified), including the bark of the cherry tree. They range from mass-produced black plastic natsume to the pristine black maki-e lacquer natsume produced over many months by master craftsmen. The best natsume often feature in museum collections, never to be used for the purpose for which they were designed and made. In the marketplace prices can range from a few pounds to many thousands, and this clearly depends on the quality, rarity and association. Mulberry wood items have a similar range in price but this is mainly related to the intrinsic wood rather than the process involved in the crafting of the object. A basic natsume in mulberry wood

76 Japanese mulberry wood thin green tea container

is shown in Illustration 74; this is claimed to be unstained wood but that is questionable given its dark brown colour. This is the classic shape for a natsume, which can be seen in a variety of different woods and lacquer finishes. Slightly more sophisticated natsume exist which are made of a standard dark-stained mulberry wood but with an inner coating of gold leaf (e.g., Illustration 38). This is both decorative and also functional because the gold does not alter or taint the taste of the powdered tea. A slightly more unusual shape is that shown in Illustration 75. This wood has not been stained and has the characteristic golden brown colour of mulberry. The lid fits perfectly and the shape is reminiscent of that found in classical ceramics. Similar classical shapes can be seen in the leaf tea caddies made of mulberry wood in Illustration 69.

Shimakuwa Tea Ceremony Items

Because the tea ceremony is an important cultural activity in Japan it is understandable that the best-quality items should be associated with it. As previously mentioned, mulberry from the Izu islands is highly regarded and this is particularly the case amongst those who work wood. The natsume in Illustration 76 is a historic example. The classically shaped natsume has a very deep, well-developed colour and is thought to have been made in the nineteenth century. The object in Illustration 54 is of a shimakuwa frame with an image associated with the tea ceremony. It shows a Geisha in traditional Japanese dress (kimono). Her hair has been dressed with ornaments in boxwood and

she is offering a chawan in a blue-and-white ceramic – probably Arita ware from Kyoto. The chawan or tea bowl is offered to a mystery guest using a special saucer made from lacquered wood or kishuware and called a Tenmokudai tea saucer. There are chopstick rests produced by Toshio Shimazaki in a standard set of five in a deep, square shimakuwa tray. These are shown in Illustration 58, which reveals the subtle and beautiful shape. Typical of Japanese design they are both restrained and functional. The same maker made the tray featured in Illustration 77.

An entirely different level of aesthetic appreciation can be seen in the shimakuwa or island mulberry items that have been specifically made for the tea ceremony. These are often signed by the maker (usually on the external box), possibly the peak of aesthetic perfection being achieved in an octagonal piece by Toshio Shimazaki (Illustration 55). The tray is made from a solid piece of shimakuwa which has been carved to create the shallow tray for the tea ceremony. The octagonal tea caddy is a tour de force of the wood worker's art – the pieces have been grain matched and joined together by invisible joints in the typical sashimono manner. The lid fits perfectly and slowly falls down the lip of the container when put in place. This is similar to a box used to store chess pieces (shogi) and shown in the 'Sashimono Furniture' television programme shown on Japanese television.[43] The sides of the form gradually taper and this makes the jointing even more skilled. The best grain was selected for the top of the tea container and this has the light and shade 'silver grain' so typical of the best golden shimakuwa island mulberry. All Toshio Shimazaki's items are finished with a fine urushi clear lacquer. These items are featured alongside a tea scoop chashaku which would be placed on the tray with the natsume during the tea ceremony. The one featured in Illustration 62, shown with a bamboo container, is of shimakuwa mulberry wood. A supreme piece of shimakuwa work by Shouji Furukawa is a tea caddy for leaf tea which has a beautifully turned recessed handled inner lid. The quality of this item is like that seen in the shimakuwa sewing cabinet in that it has a very fine border lip around the finished edges. This is characteristic of most high-quality furniture and wooden items in Japan.

The Game of Go and Moku/Tamamoku Knots

Go originated in China and spread to both Japan and Korea. It is a game of skill and tactics and is based around a grid or board and black and white stones. Fundamentally, the game is territorial and is a competition between two people, although there are Go groups or associations throughout the world. Go has a number of objects associated with it which have a rich heritage.

There are three main components of the game beginning with the board, which is one very thick and solid piece of quality wood. The best are made from kaya wood (*Torreya nucifera*), which like shimakuwa can come from trees over 500 years old that tend to grow in the Miyazaki prefecture in Japan. The kaya boards can be classified into two further types: a bent and irregular grain called itame and a straight-running grain called masame. The masame type boards can be further classified depending on the flow of the grain. The best boards can be very expensive and the finest quality boards tend to have very high-quality Go bowls to match. These are often made of Mikura island mulberry or shimakuwa (Illustration 60) and can be classified into different types dependent on the grain and knots. Those with beautiful knots (Go bowls come in pairs) are called the moku type and the rarest type is called tamamoku, which has the finest patterned knots. Like all shimakuwa these bowls tend to have the dual grain, which has a shimmering character. There are two bowls because there are two types of stones, made of slate and shell. Again, the source of these is important, with the best black slate coming from Wakayama prefecture, while the best white shell stones are made from clam shells that are processed on the island of Kyushu. A very high-quality game set can cost over a million yen and half of the cost can be due to the shimakuwa bowls. Lower-grade mulberry bowls can be purchased like the bowl featured in Illustration 78 which is simply made of mountain mulberry.[44]

77 Japanese mulberry wood tea ceremony set in shimakuwa

Mingei and Kokten Korgei

Religion plays an important part in the everyday life of the Japanese, particularly the philosophy of Buddhism and its Zen aspect. The impact of Zen has featured in virtually every aspect of art and culture, including interiors, gardens, aesthetics and the tea ceremony. Both Shinto shrines and Buddhist temples can be found throughout Japan and both religions have an intrinsic association with nature and the naturalistic. This means that in both religions trees are revered and respected. The wood from trees is as a consequence highly regarded and this is particularly true of the mulberry tree because it is so productive. In his essay in *Crafting Beauty in Modern Japan*, Kaneko Kenji recognises four distinct tendencies concerning the development of craft in Japan at the start of the twentieth century:

1. Those who strove to transform themselves from artisan to artist based on Western styles and philosophies.
2. Those who revived classical Chinese and Korean ceramic styles.
3. Those who sought to revive classical Japanese styles of the past.
4. Those who worked in a folk craft tradition, with all the associated philosophies.[45]

The last tendency has the greatest integrity and this is the one which has been developed so successfully in the twentieth century. The connection of skill with the craft tradition of everyday objects was under scrutiny after the implementation of factory production in Japan. Soetsu Yanagi (1889–1961) was concerned about the loss of skills relating to production and tried to promote a resurgence in simple but beautiful objects for everyday life or ordinary people's art. As a result of this a museum was set up in 1936 at Komaba, Tokyo called the Japan Folk Crafts Museum (Nihon Mingeikan). This acted as a prototype for others in Japan and abroad, including the Mingei International Museum of World Folk Art located in San Diego, California. In 1995 this museum displayed a comparative exhibition of American Shaker production and the arts of everyday life in Japan, with an accompanying catalogue. Author June Sprigg cites Soetsu Yanagi as an important influence, and says of Shaker and Japanese aesthetics:

> When I consider Shaker design now, I think of the dry Zen garden of Ryoan-ji in Kyoto – fifteen rocks placed in a sea of raked gravel by a monk some 500 years ago. It seems utterly straightforward, until we learn that one of the rocks is always concealed by another from our point of view as we circle the plot, no matter where we stand. Those who would see all fifteen rocks must free themselves from the bonds of this world and the limitations

78 Japanese mulberry wood Go bowl with lid

79 Japanese mulberry tree bonsai in terracotta dish

of time and space. I think that Hannah Cohoon, the Shaker sister and vision artist who painted 'The Tree of Life' bowing and blowing in the celestial wind of the realm of the spirit, would have understood clearly what I see.[46]

This karesansui dry rock garden is part of a world heritage site and featured as Garden 42 in the television series *Around the World in 80 Gardens*, presented by Monty Don.[47] Hannah Cohoon (1788–1864) featured abstract mulberry trees in her visionary work *A Bower of Mulberry Trees* produced in 1854.[48]

In the Mingei exhibition catalogue Martha Longenecker mentions Dr Soetsu Yanagi, who has been a resident of the USA and was a lecturer at Harvard University. She writes:

He observed that many articles made by unknown craftsmen of pre-industrialised times were of a beauty seldom equalled by artists of modern societies. He recognised that unsurpassed beauty was the flowering of a unified expression when there is no division of head, heart and hands and that, with the increasing mechanisation of society, few people perform an act of total attention. Sori, the son of Soetsu, has directed the Japan Folk Crafts Museum so the family (like craftspeople) are passing down the heritage. Sori has stated: 'Tread not in the footsteps of the past, but seek what they sought.'[49] In *The Art of Japanese Craft* exhibition catalogue, Kaneko Kenji writes: 'The tea ceremony provided another cultural continuity to which Japanese craftsmen could look, transforming traditional tea paraphernalia into modern craft art.'[50]

There are craftspeople who have used the past as a source of inspiration for their contemporary work and this is very much the case with Kichizo and its mulberry furniture range. The concern for taking influence from past traditions can be found in the society called Kokten Korgei. Blackwell, the Arts and Crafts house designed by Baillie Scott (1865–1945), was an entirely appropriate location for an exhibition of mainly Japanese work based around Kokten Korgei, including work in ceramics, paper, glass, wood, lacquer and textiles (including some beautiful ikat pieces). Both Mingei and Kokten Korgei are connected and their history has been detailed in the *Japanese Craft Tradition* catalogue.[51] The essence of both movements is centred on the making process, applied skill and aesthetic considerations. The beauty of all the objects is that they can be used – they have a purpose and function, the form following the function.

Conclusion

Ritual and custom have been discussed in this chapter with specific reference to the tea ceremony in Japan. The influence of religion in Japan, particularly Shinto, on the design and making process is significant. In the *British Museum Souvenir Guide* (2009), in the section on Japan, we read:

> Shinto, 'the way of the gods', was one of the strongest influences on the development of Japanese culture: with its emphasis on love and respect for the natural world, ancestors and craftsmanship, and on the inseparability of the physical and the spiritual, it played a large role in the adaptation and reinterpretation of ideas and techniques received from the mainland.[52]

The mulberry tree in Japan is highly respected because of its functionality, and trees such as the ones growing on the Izu islands have a further importance because they are ancient. Interestingly, whilst mulberry trees are commonplace and associated with the silk industry, trees located naturally in the wild are relatively rare. Often, mass-planted, silk-production mulberry trees are pollarded so that the leaves can be readily harvested. In Japan (unlike the United Kingdom) it is very rare to find mulberry trees in garden settings. However, they are occasionally used in the creation of bonsai, such as the one exported to the United Kingdom and shown in Illustration 79. In the Winterthur catalogue, *Seeing Things Differently*, it states: 'Objects contribute significantly to the practice of many daily routines, as well as the enactment of special occasions. When used to perform various social tasks or to give shape to the physical setting, they may acquire additional layers of meaning.'[53] The objects created from mulberry for the tea ceremony have these layers relating both to the aesthetics of the objects, which are often simple but beautifully made, and to the social interaction of the ceremony for tea which involves a complex series of actions and processes.

Tea drinking has a ritual in the United Kingdom specifically in the form of afternoon tea, but the ceremony in Japan is on an entirely different level. Afternoon tea has become fashionable again in the United Kingdom, whilst most people in Japan have never really experienced an authentic tea ceremony. The objects created for the tea ceremony do not have as much cultural resonance in contemporary Japan, as social patterns and interactions have changed in the modern world. Some of the objects created for the purpose of the ceremony are never going to be used because they are in museums or private collections. Tea can now be prepared in less than two minutes, is vended from a machine and consumed both hot and cold. Fruit and herbal teas have become popular and there is even a mulberry tea made from the leaves of the tree that has medicinal properties.

The truly beautiful wood called shimakuwa has become a rarity and has in fact been pronounced 'the rarest wood in the world'.[54] Not only has the wood become difficult to obtain but the skills involved in the making of objects in the craft tradition are also declining (or have vanished) in contemporary Japan.[55] Objects created by current makers in Japan using shimakuwa have ironically now become far more defined by art than design – they appear in exhibitions alongside critiques and are purely for looking at rather than using. Sadly, something has been lost when this happens: items become artefacts rather than designed and crafted objects for daily use; they are no longer in an honest Mingei tradition.

Notes to Chapter 4

1   *Japanese Crafts: A Complete Guide*, p. 14.

2   Ibid.

3   Catalogue for the *Age of Experience* exhibition, curated by Mary La Trobe-Bateman, at Ruthin Craft Centre, Lon Parcwr, Wales (2009). See 'Biographies' section (p. 54).

4   Okamura Kichiemon, *Japanese Ikat* (Kyoto: Fujioka Mamoru, Kyoto Shoin Co., 1993).

5   Rousmaniere, *Crafting Beauty in Modern Japan*, p. 160.

6   *The Japanese Craft Tradition: Kokten Korgei*, with a foreword by Edward King and an essay by Professor Samiro Yunoki (Bowness-on-Windermere: Lakeland Arts Trust, 2001). This was a catalogue to accompany an exhibition at Blackwell, The Arts and Crafts House, Bowness-on-Windermere, Cumbria, 3 October–21 December 2001.

7   See n. 3, above.

8   Ruth Pavey, 'Sources of Inspiration: Mary Restieaux', *Crafts* (July–August 2002), pp. 37–39.

9   Russell and Cohn, *Izu Islands*.

10 See Bowett, *Woods in British Furniture Making, 1400–1900*, p. 158.

11 See www.tunbridgewellsmuseum.org/default.aspx?page=1643 (accessed 20 November 2012).

12 *David Linley Gifts and Accessories Catalogue, 2011–2012* (London: David Linley, 2011). See the illustration on p. 40.

13 See www.davidlinley.com (accessed 14 August 2012).

14 Victor H. Mair and Erling Hoh, *The True History of Tea* (London: Thames & Hudson, 2009), p. 173.

15 *Japanese Crafts: A Complete Guide*, p. 108.

16 See www.awagami.com (accessed 22 October 2012).

17 Bruce Altshuler, *Isamu Noguchi (Modern Masters)* (New York: Abbeville Press, 1995).

18 Illustration 72. Vitra catalogue for Isamu Noguchi Akari Light Sculptures: Vitra Design Museum (2008). Sourced from Vitra Ltd, London.

19 Altshuler, *Isamu Noguchi*.

20 See www.noguchi.org, particularly the article by Bruce Altshuler on Akari lights (accessed 22 October 2012).

21 Helen B. Chapin, 'Themes of the Japanese Netsuke Carver', *The Art Bulletin: An Illustrated Quarterly*, 5.1 (1922) (The College Art Association of America), pp. 10–21 (p. 12).

22 Raymond Bushell, *Inro Handbook* (Tokyo: Weatherhill Inc., 1990).

23 Julia Hutt, *Japanese Netsuke*, with a foreword by Edmund de Waal (London: V&A Publications, 2012). The bean pods feature on p. 30, whilst the persimmon is on p. 89 and pumpkin on p. 94.

24 See www.antiqueNETSUKE.co.uk (accessed 12 June 2012).

25 Neil MacGregor, *A History of the World in 100 Objects* (book), p. 59.

26 Seno Tanaka and Sendo Tanaka, *The Tea Ceremony* (Tokyo: Kodansha International, 1998), pp. 207–212.

27 Sadako Ohki, *Tea Culture of Japan*, with a contribution by Takeshi Watanabe (New Haven, Conn.: Yale University Art Gallery, 2009). This accompanied an exhibition entitled *Tea Culture of Japan: Chanoyu Past and Present*, which ran from 20 January to 26 April 2009. See the illustrations on pp. 30 and 31 (Figures 1 and 2).

28 Jean M. Burks, *Shaker Design: Out of this World* (New Haven, Conn.: Yale University Press, 2008), p. 237. This publication accompanied an exhibition at the Bard Graduate Center for Studies in the Decorative Arts, Design and Culture, New York entitled *Out of this World: Shaker Design Past, Present, and Future*, which ran from 13 March to 15 June 2008.

29 Calza, *Japan Style*, p. 14 in the section 'Tea and the Aesthetics of the Undefined'.

30 Ohki, *Tea Culture of Japan*, p. 13.

31 Mair and Hoh, *The True History of Tea*.

32 Tanaka and Tanaka, *The Tea Ceremony*, pp. 193–196.

33 Mair and Hoh, *The True History of Tea*, p. 100.

34 Okakura Kakuzo, *The Book of Tea*, with an afterword by Jim Massey (Philadelphia, Pa.: Running Press, 2002).

35 Tanaka and Tanaka, *The Tea Ceremony*, p. 134.

36 See Monty Don, *Around the World in 80 Gardens* (London: Weidenfeld & Nicolson, 2008). Produced alongside a television series for BBC2, first broadcast in 2008, and produced in a four DVD box set by Warner Home Video.

37 Chris Caldicott, 'Discover: The Gardens of Japan', *Homes & Gardens*, May 2012, pp. 201–204.

38 Morgan Pitelka, *Japanese Tea Culture: Art, History and Practice* (London: Routledge, 2003). With specific reference to the chapter 'Tea Records'.

39 See www.christineannrichards.co.uk (accessed 3 September 2012).

40 See Koizumi, *Traditional Japanese Furniture*, p. 123.

41 See Rousmaniere, *Crafting Beauty in Modern Japan*, p. 126.

42 Tanaka and Tanaka, *The Tea Ceremony*, p. 65.

43 'Sashimono Furniture' in the NHK World television series, *Begin Japanology*.

44 www.kiseido.com (accessed 2 November 2012).

45 Kaneko Kenji, 'The Development of "Traditional Crafts" in Japan', in Rousmaniere, *Crafting Beauty in Modern Japan*, pp. 10 and 11. Information taken from p. 10.

46 June Sprigg, Prologue, in Burks, *Shaker Design*, pp. 9–14 (p. 13).

47 Don, *Around the World in 80 Gardens*.

48 Hannah Cohoon, *A Bower of Mulberry Trees* (1854), in the collections of Hancock Shaker Museum, Massachusetts.

49 *Kindred Spirits: The Eloquence of Function in American Shaker and Japanese Arts of Daily Life*, with a foreword by Martha W. Longenecker (San Diego, Calif.: Mingei International Museum, 1995), p. 16.

50 Fischer, *The Art of Japanese Craft*, p. 11.

51 *The Japanese Craft Tradition: Kokten Korgei*, with a foreword by Edward King and an essay by Professor Samiro Yunoki.

52 *The British Museum Souvenir Guide* (London: British Museum Press, 2009), p. 46.

53 Graves, *Seeing Things Differently*, p. 56.

54 See www.Japaneseartsandcrafts (accessed 3 October 2012).

55 Michael Kleindl, 'Master Craftsman Carries on *Sashimono* Tradition', *Japanese Times*, 4 May 2013: www.japantimes.co.jp/community/2013/05/04/our-lives/master-craftsman-carries-on-sashimono-tradition/ (accessed 3 September 2013).

80 American Watson
Box at the Winterthur
Museum
By permission of the
Winterthur Museum

Messages and Symbols

Introduction

The Winterthur catalogue, *Seeing Things Differently*, states:

> Objects possess layers of meaning. Investigating their design, construction, uses in the household, and roles in larger social, economic, and cultural networks opens these layers to historical interpretation. In addition, some objects also may be understood through the specific messages or ideas they were meant to convey. Indeed, in some objects, the specific message function is so strong that it obscures everything else about the object.[1]

This is the case with certain artefacts and stories related to the mulberry tree. It features in a number of different mythologies, including Chinese, Roman and Greek tales. Perhaps the most famous is the Ovidian version of a legend featuring Pyramus and Thisbe. It is based on a story of lovers living in the Mesopotamian city of Babylon. They arrange to meet under the shade of a mulberry tree. Thisbe arrives first but she drops her scarf in her rush. Because Pyramus is not there she departs, but a lion with a bloodstained mouth finds the scarf and stains it with some blood. Pyramus arrives at the mulberry tree but finds only the scarf; assuming the worst he kills himself in grief. Thisbe returns and tragically finds the dead body of Pyramus and in distress she also kills herself. The gods in an act of memorialisation change the mulberry tree berries from white to a deep blood red.

Thisbe features in a 1909 Pre-Raphaelite painting by John William Waterhouse (1849–1917) and she is mentioned by Jeremiah Holmes Wiffen (1792–1836) in a poem written in 1824. Wiffen pressed a leaf from the Milton mulberry tree at Cambridge into a gift copy of a first edition of his book, *The Works of Garcilasso de la Vega*, which was gifted to Arcisse de Caumont.[2] It is said that Shakespeare used the story of Pyramus and Thisbe as a source for some of his plays, including *Romeo and Juliet* and *A Midsummer Night's Dream* and there is a thread of connection between mulberry trees and Shakespeare that runs further than these plays, as we will see later. This chapter is really about the connections – literary and scientific – between people and the black mulberry tree, *Morus nigra*.

Messages and Literature – More, Milton and Morris

Defying numerous attempts – over a dozen unsuccessful letters, emails and telephone communications – the most elusive mulberry tree in this study was the one located in the grounds of Allen Hall, a Roman Catholic seminary in the diocese of Westminster, London. The motto for the college is 'We Live in Hope' and that was the abiding sensation obtained from the efforts to obtain any information from the institution regarding its mulberry tree. Much of the background detail had to be obtained from its website.[3] It was only in 1975 that the seminary moved to the great house of Saint Thomas More and the mulberry tree in the grounds is said to have been planted by More himself, making it one of the oldest in the United Kingdom. A plaque by the tree reads:

> This famous old mulberry tree
> bound together by cross bands
> and chains dates back to the time
> of Saint Thomas More – Lord
> Chancellor under King Henry
> VIII. He was beheaded in 1535
> in defence of the Catholic faith.
> When surrounded by his family
> and friends it is certain he often
> held those witty and tender
> conversations which he loved
> beneath its shelter.

Thomas More was canonised in 1935. He was apparently interested in mulberry trees and, like the More-Molyneux family, to whom he was related, he wanted a connection because of the *Morus* name and the numerous puns associated with the word.[4] The old mulberry tree found in the seminary is beautifully shaped and located quite near to the building. A selection of younger trees have also been planted as part of a Saint Thomas More mulberry walk. There are a small number of extant portraits of More and one exceptional painting, by Hans Holbein, features in the Frick Collection, New York. More's life has been extensively documented, from *The Life of Sir Thomas More*, written by William Roper (1496–1578), apparently during the reign of Queen Mary (1553–1558), to more contemporary accounts.[5] He is the first of three examples of learned men being pictured under the shade of a mulberry tree – Thomas More (1478–1535), John Milton (1608–1674) and William Morris (1834–1896).

The present study was initiated because of the fascinating episode of a television programme called *Meetings with Remarkable Trees* on Milton's mulberry, mentioned in Chapter 1,[6] although the black mulberry associated with Christ's College, Cambridge (Survey List 7) and John Milton is not featured in the accompanying book and audiobook. There is a portrait *c*.1629 of poet John Milton by an unknown artist in the National Portrait Gallery.[7] Some have even suggested that he wrote the pastoral elegy *Lycidas* under the shade of the mulberry tree. There is a blue plaque in Bread Street, London to mark the place where he was born and his early education was at St Paul's School. He graduated with a BA from Cambridge University in 1629 and the university has many recorded associations with the writer. In an essay by Charles Lesingham Smith, a Fellow of Christ's College, entitled 'Milton's Mulberry Tree', and first published in 1840, we read:

> On a small grass-plot at the
> extremity of the gardens of
> Christ's College there grows a
> very remarkable decrepit old
> mulberry tree. One glimpse is
> sufficient to convince the most
> incurious observer that this tree
> is not as other trees are. Its age
> is marked out, not so much by its
> size, which is rather diminutive,
> as by the sturdy proportion of its
> limbs; by their almost invariably
> striking off from each other at
> right angles.[8]

In the piece it is claimed that the old tree was associated with John Milton and there is a tradition among the Fellows of Christ's College, which can never be entirely proven, that it was planted during Milton's time at Cambridge. In some archival material this has been disputed – for example, a diary preserved amongst the Bowtell manuscripts suggests that the tree was blown down in a hurricane in 1795 and that it was likely (by conjecture) that the tree was planted via the James I edict of 1609. In fact, Dr Geoff Baldwin, a Fellow in History at Christ's, suggests that it was planted around the time of Milton's birth in 1608 and that the college purchased 300 mulberries from the Stuart king.[9]

Milton had a number of other connections with mulberry trees, one being the tree found in Stowmarket (Survey List 69) and another the tree at Milton's Cottage, Chalfont St Giles (Survey List 88). In the case of Stowmarket the connection with Milton relates to the fact that his tutor, the Revd Thomas Young, was vicar there when Milton visited him in 1628. It is thought likely that the tree was planted around this time. It was blown down in 1939 but has survived via re-growth as the tree that stands outside the Stowmarket Town Council offices today. Whilst some have indicated that the tree's origins are in the eighteenth century, it would appear that no actual detailed information exists. Another resident of the Milton vicarage in the Victorian period was the Revd A. G. H. Hollingsworth, who produced a history of Stowmarket. He liked to think that the epitaph of the Revd Thomas Young was written by Milton: 'Here is committed to earth's trust – wise, pious, spotlesse, learned dust.' The mulberry tree was famous during the Victorian period for the copious amounts of juice produced from the fruit – this being processed into a considerable amount of wine.

The other Milton-related mulberry tree is located at Milton's Cottage in Chalfont St Giles in Buckinghamshire. The association with Milton is that he visited the village in 1665 in order to escape the plague which was evident in London. The tree is a descendant of the one at Christ's College but is a relatively young specimen. Other progeny of the tree at Cambridge have also found various homes, a particularly appropriate one being reported by BBC news on 18 May 2008: a mulberry sapling was planted to celebrate the 400th anniversary of Milton's birth, in Drovers Wood, Upper Breinton, which is located by the Hay literary site. This coincided with a talk by the Milton biographer Mary Beer at what was the twenty-first festival. Further

celebrations of this anniversary included a special exhibition at Cambridge University.

John Blatchly's article in the *East Anglian Daily Times* tells the story of two trees, the first at Christ's College and the second at Stowmarket, and the article also has two colour photographs of the trees in their contemporary settings.[10] Both trees are tourist attractions and the fruit continues to be collected; in the case of the tree at Cambridge, the resultant harvest is made into jam for the college and for visitors to purchase. It states in the television programme 'Milton's Mulberry', in the resonant voiceover by Bill Paterson: 'To the college the Milton mulberry is much more than a relic to James I's ill-conceived silk industry. This venerable old tree is venue for reflection, recital and music – and is set to stay a focal point of college life for generations of students to come.'[11] There is a sculptural portrait of Milton (as part of a paper knife and clip) carved out of a piece of mulberry wood in the Pinto collection housed at Birmingham City Museums (Illustration 23).[12] Along with other objects in the collection it could possibly have been made from Shakespeare's mulberry tree (see below).

Another learned and literary man associated with a mulberry tree was William Morris. Morris was linked with the Red House, Bexleyheath (1859) and with Kelmscott Manor (Survey List 1), which he rented from 1869. Kelmscott is of particular interest to this study because it is the location of a beautiful old black mulberry tree. The building is Grade I listed whilst the gardens are included in the English Heritage Register of Historic Parks and Gardens (1998).

The gardens at Kelmscott are thought to have been a direct inspiration to Morris in the creation of his patterns for both wallpapers and fabrics. This part of Morris's productive life was featured in a book produced to celebrate the 150th anniversary of the company Morris & Co.[13] The firm was established by Morris alongside Ford Maddox Brown (1821–1893), Dante Gabriel Rossetti (1828–1882), Edward Burne-Jones (1833–1898), Peter Paul Marshall (1830–1900), Charles James Faulkner (1833–1892) and Philip Webb (1831–1915). The book features many of the traditional designs by the company, including Willow Bough, which was designed and created in 1887 and has been in continuous production ever since.[14] The beautiful original drawing/watercolour is in the collections of the Whitworth Art Gallery, Manchester and featured in the exhibition *William Morris: A Sense of Place* held at Blackwell, The Arts and Crafts House.[15] In 2011, the company produced a series of fabrics, including an elaborate Kelmscott

81 American white mulberry wood, mulberry leaf carving, by Janel Jacobson

Tree machine embroidery based on bed curtains at Kelmscott Manor that were embroidered by William Morris's daughter May (1862–1938) in 1891. In the same year, William Morris produced a limited edition (300) Kelmscott Press book bound in vellum with green silk ties entitled *Poems By The Way*.[16] This featured the mulberry tree in the poem 'Tapestry Trees', in the section *Verses for Pictures*: 'Love's lack hath dyed my berries red: For Love's attire my leaves are shed'. The mulberry is also mentioned in 'The Flowering Orchard: Silk Embroidery':

> Lo silken my garden, and silken
> my sky,
> And silken my apple-boughs
> hanging on high;
> All wrought by the Worm in the
> peasant carle's cot
> On the Mulberry leafage when
> summer was hot![17]

Describing Morris's novel *News from Nowhere*, Alan Crossley, Tom Hassall and Peter Salway write that the book 'is suffused with Morris's love of the countryside, landscape and field archaeology'.[18] In her biography of Morris, Fiona MacCarthy graphically charts the development of these interests through Morris's boyhood spent on the fringes of Epping Forest.[19]

Morris was instrumental in the formation of the Society for the Protection of Ancient Buildings and Kelmscott Manor is now preserved under the auspices of the Society of Antiquaries of London. The Society has produced a guidebook to the property and the garden features heavily in the book, which charts its development through the extensive restoration process:

> To the north west of the house
> there was an orchard, which
> was created in 1995 and is now
> planted with old apple trees
> (Blenheim Orange, Gascoyne's
> Scarlet, Lady Sudeley, King of
> the Pippins, Adam's Pearmain,
> American Mother and Beauty of
> Bath). To the west of the house
> there is a fine old mulberry
> tree. Around this tree paths and
> flowerbeds have been created.
> The orchard is divided from the
> flowerbeds by a rustic pole fence
> with roses along it. All these fea-
> tures reproduce the appearance
> indicated by photos taken in May
> Morris's day.[20]

A photograph shows the west garden in spring which features the black mulberry tree without

82 English mulberry wood Shakespeare snuff box

leaves and the tree is accompanied by other traditional species including crab apples, willow, walnut, horse chestnut and black poplar (*Populus nigra*).[21]

Philip Webb was a friend of Morris's and the architect associated with the Red House. He created a simple but beautiful tombstone for Morris which is located in St Georges Churchyard at Kelmscott. Webb also designed a pair of memorial cottages for William Morris's wife Jane (1839–1914) and these have a stone sculptural panel on the front which features Morris sitting under trees – one of which is the black mulberry tree (with associated blackbirds). This was carved by George Jack in 1902 from a sketch by Webb. It is unlikely that a better vision of Morris exists and it encapsulates what William Morris was about. In July 2012, the William Morris Gallery in Walthamstow (Morris's home from 1848 to 1856) was reopened after refurbishment and featured in its temporary gallery the Walthamstow Tapestry by Grayson Perry. This was reviewed in the *Daily Telegraph*[22] and the entire tapestry features on the Factum Arte website.[23]

Symbols and Literature – Cowper and Shakespeare

William Cowper (1731–1800) wrote in *The Task* (1785): 'And from his touchwood trunk the mulb'ry tree supplied such relics as devotion holds. Still sacred, and preserves with pious care.' This quotation refers to Shakespeare and appeared on an information board in an exhibition called *Fakes, Forgeries & Facsimiles* held at the Folger Shakespeare Library, Washington, DC,[24] which in part referenced Shakespeare's mulberry tree *memento mori*. It further stated on the exhibition board:

> Thus Cowper described the mulberry tree that gave birth to the Shakespeare relic industry. Supposedly planted by Shakespeare himself, the tree grew in his former garden until 1756 when it was sold for firewood. Instead of burning it, purchasers transformed the firewood into saleable items and made a fortune. The issue of fakery has several dimensions here. Did Shakespeare actually plant the tree? Was a particular item marked 'Shakespeare's wood' actually made from the mulberry tree cut down in 1756? Was the wood even genuine mulberry? Did wood from trees grown from slips of the original mulberry count as genuine? The only certainty, as a modern scholar observed, is that the tree provided a 'new and strange addition to rural England's arts and crafts, namely that of making poetry pay'.

William Cowper was born in Berkhamstead in Hertfordshire and throughout his life suffered periods of melancholia. An evangelical religious convert, he was responsible for writing the *Olney Hymns* (1779) in collaboration with the Revd John Newton (1725–1807) as well as various literary works including *The Task*. He was most famous perhaps for being a letter writer – a skill which has been virtually lost in the digital age. Some of these letters feature in *William Cowper: The Centenary Letters*, which was produced in association with the Cowper Museum at Orchard Side, Olney, Milton Keynes.[25]

Much of the environment at Cowper's Olney home has been preserved as part of the Cowper and Newton Museum. This contains artefacts, portraits and a family tree alongside interpretive material on his life and works. Curiously there is one object in the collections which is interesting because it is made of mulberry wood. The object, described as a watch stand, was apparently made of wood sourced from a mulberry tree which had grown in the Olney orchard garden. Perhaps the mulberry tree was originally grown as a tribute to William Shakespeare from one writer to another? The watch stand is displayed in a glazed cabinet by the entrance to the parlour from the hall.[26] Sadly, Cowper's final work remained unfinished because of ill health; it was intended to be based on John Milton's poetry with proposed illustrations by Henry Fuseli (1741–1825). The company Tiptree, which makes mulberry jam, has advertised on television using a series of quotations, including one by William Cowper.[27]

Another literary figure with a significant association with mulberry trees is William Shakespeare (1564–1616). As previously mentioned, a whole relic industry has developed around his persona and features in both private and museum collections throughout the world. For example, there is a collection of the letters and artefacts of Jane Catherine Gamble (1810–1885) in the Girton College archives at Cambridge University[28] covering the period 1783 to 1874. It includes correspondence with authors, artists and scientists, and, significantly, all these items are contained within a wooden box said to be made of wood from the mulberry tree planted by William Shakespeare. An authenticating note reads:

> Note (with plain outer cover) signed 'Thomas Rackett July 30 1832' to authenticate the provenance of Jane Catherine Gamble's wooden box. The box which accompanies this Paper was made out of the Mulberry Tree planted by Shakespeare, a part of which was found in the possession of Mrs Garrick (by myself and Mr Beltz her Executors) duly authenticated and sealed at each end as originally received by Mr Garrick. The light coloured wood is part of the Cypress Tree planted at Hampton by Mr & Mrs Garrick. The seal with the letters W S is from a ring/seal found about 15 years ago at Stratford upon Avon. There is great reason to believe this ring belonged to the Immortal Bard.

There was an exhibition at the National Portrait Gallery, London in 2006 with the title *Searching for Shakespeare*. The catalogue features such a ring as described above, and its questionable provenance is discussed as follows:

> Since its discovery in 1810, there

has been much speculation that the ring might have belonged to William Shakespeare. In a letter to John Keats (1795–1821), the artist Robert Haydon (1786–1846), who was convinced of the authenticity of ownership, wrote: 'I certainly go mad! In a field at Stratford upon Avon, in a field that belonged to Shakespeare; they have found a gold ring and seal, with initials thus – W.S. and a true lover's knot!! As sure as you breathe, & he that was the first of beings the Seal belonged to him – Oh Lord!'[29]

This Gamble box appears very similar to the Watson box in the collections at Winterthur (Illustration 80), which has a series of relics and artefacts which have significance beyond their material worth because of their attached histories, stories and messages. Both the Gamble box and the Watson box contain artefacts relating to American presidents, and a contemporary item with a similar story is the piece named *Ark of the Founders*, which featured in an exhibition called *National Treasures* at the Ohio Craft Museum.[30] This piece used various historic woods, including material from a horse chestnut (*Aesculus hippocastanum*) planted by George Washington and also a George Washington era mulberry wood sample (*Morus alba*) from Mount Vernon shaped into an okimono or netsuke like a mulberry leaf (Illustration 81). Another Shakespeare memento appears in the collections of General Grant's House and Library, New York and the wooden box has an inscription which indicates that it was made from mulberry wood thought to have been sourced from the tree planted by Shakespeare at New Place, Stratford-upon-Avon.

In Washington, DC, the Folger Shakespeare Library has many items related to William Shakespeare's mulberry tree, including a magnificent tea caddy (Museum Number ART Inv. 1111) from the late eighteenth century, reputed to have been made by Thomas Sharp (1724–1799). The caddy displays carvings of branches from a mulberry tree showing both fruits and leaves with a plaque portrait of Shakespeare after the Chandos image. There are numerous examples of mulberry wood tea caddies, including one in the collections of the V&A. The caddy (Museum Number W16 1881) is thought to be by George Cooper (dated 1759) and the museum acquired it by auction from the Prescott collection (Lot 74, Christie's, New York, 31 January

1981). A similar tea caddy to the one in the V&A was recorded for sale at Sotheby's, London in 2000.[31] The caddy (Lot 1) was made in 1759 by George Cooper and was described thus: 'the rectangular lid with a brass swing handle, carved with a coat of arms, fruiting mulberry branches and geometric designs against a punched background, the front edge with a carved bust of Shakespeare'. Of George Cooper, it says:

> Born in Stratford in 1720, very little is recorded of George Cooper until 1759 when his name is mentioned by the antiquarian John Jordon in his later account of the mulberry tree story. He includes Cooper's name amongst the buyers of the uprooted mulberry tree, together with the comment that he was a 'poor joiner of Stratford, whose curiosity excited him to work what little he was able to purchase into tots, such as tea chests, boxes and tobacco stoppers etc., some of which were prettily carved'.

Robert Bearman's recent examination of contemporary documents has revealed that soon after buying the wood Cooper's business was taken over by the silversmith Thomas Sharp, who we now know employed Cooper as assistant, raising the possibility that the mulberry wood carvings hitherto attributed to Sharp may in fact have been made by Cooper.

Possibly the best UK collection of artefacts related to the mulberry tree in Shakespeare's garden is appropriately located at the Shakespeare Birthplace Trust, Stratford-upon-Avon. The collection comprises various items, including a snuff box (Museum Number SBT 2003-12), raw wood, busts, goblets, inkstands, boxes, tea caddies, smoking ephemera, rosary beads and a phial containing mulberry juice thought to have originated from the fruit of the mulberry tree planted by Shakespeare. The object (Museum Number SBT 1868-3/87) has an inscription on an attached label which states: 'This juice was made of some mulberries gathered from the tree planted by the renowned poet William Shakespeare by my mother who gave it to me on the 29th June, 1774 (Philip Wren).'

Many of these objects are extensively catalogued and appear in the archive and also on the website of the museum. A significant number of items are thought to have originated from Thomas Sharp. In addition, there are also objects thought to have been made by Cooper, including a bust of William Shakespeare (Museum

83 Black mulberry botanic illustration, by William Hooker
By permission of the Royal Horticultural Society

The Black Mulberry.

Number SBT 1999-2), which has an ink-written inscription on the base: 'memento mori/ Remember ye mulberry tree/Shakespeare's Jubilee at Stratford on Avon 1769'.

The Folger Shakespeare Library's very extensive collection of mulberry items includes an array of objects from the relatively large to the very small, including raw wood, goblets, a tobacco box, a thimble case, a rolling pin, various containers and an inkstand carved with mulberry leaves and berries (Museum Number ART inv. 1125; sc 1985). Again, this collection is extensively catalogued with detailed notes on provenance and summary reports. The name Thomas Sharp appears regularly across both the Stratford-upon-Avon and Washington catalogues and it looks as if he was central in creating the objects associated with William Shakespeare's mulberry tree. In fact, in the archives at the Folger Shakespeare Library there is a letter from the Trustees and Guardians of Shakespeare's Birthplace, Stratford-upon-Avon, dated 2 July 1928, in which they forwarded a sworn declaration by Thomas Sharp confirming the authenticity of the mulberry wood that was connected with William Shakespeare. It reads:

> This is to certify that I Thos. Sharp of the Borough of Stratford upon Avon in the County of Warwick, Clerk and Watchmaker was born in the Chapel Street & Baptised Feb. 5th 1724, that I was personally acquainted with Sir Hugh Clopton Knight Barrister at Law and one of the Heralds at Arms who was son of Sir John Clopton Knight that purchased a certain Messuage or House near to the Chapel in Stratford called the new Place of the Executors of Lacy Elizabeth Barnard and Granddaughter of Shakespeare & that I have often heard the said Sir Hugh Clopton solemnly declare that the Mulberry Tree which growed in his Garden was planted by Shakespeare and he took pride in shewing it to & entertaining Persons of distinction whose curiosity excited them to visit the Spot known to be the last Residence of the immortal Bard and after the Disease of the said Sir Hugh in 1753 the premises were sold to the Rev. Jno Gastrell who in 1756 cut down the said Mulberry tree and cleft it as firewood when the greatest part of it was purchased by me the said Thos. Sharp who out of sincere veneration for the memory of its celebrated planter employed one John Lackman to convey it to my premise where I have worked it into many curious Toys and useful articles from the same and I hereby declare & take my solemn oath upon the four Evangelists in the presence of Almighty God that I never had worked sold or substituted any other Wood than what came from & was part of the self Tree signed and a true Affidavit made by me (with a signature Thos. Sharp).

An article by John Hardy, entitled 'Ryland's "Shakespeare Wood" Tea Caddy', reiterates the story:

> A fine mulberry tree in the 'sacred ground which the Muses had consecrated to the memory of their favourite poet' was planted according to its owner Sir Hugh Clopton (d. 1751), by the hand of Shakespeare himself in 1609. This caused it to join the poet's monument in Holy Trinity Church as an object to veneration for scholars, poets and thespians, such as David Garrick (1717–1779), who made his pilgrimage to New Place shortly after his debut on the London stage in 1742.[32]

An account featuring Shakespeare, the mulberry tree and 'bardolatry', alongside discussion of Thomas Sharp, George Cooper and John Marshall, can be found in a recent edition of *Antique Collecting*.[33] The article attempts to contextualise the origins of the mementos that were created and tries to explain how they became so sought after and collectable. However, it does not really give a rational explanation as to how so many objects (some of considerable size) were created from just one mulberry tree. A scientific analysis of the objects would prove interesting and would probably reveal some fakery – but if the majority proved to be made out of mulberry it would be almost impossible to disprove their origins.

One person above all others could be said to have been the main protagonist in the creation of the 'bard brand' and that is David Garrick. He was an actor at the Theatre

Royal, Drury Lane who took on the management of the site, promoting Shakespeare to contemporary audiences by acting in and presenting Shakespeare's plays and Shakespearean events. He was instrumental in celebrating Shakespeare with a jubilee event and festivities in 1769 that had the cooperation of the Stratford-upon-Avon town council. According to John Hardy:

> The jubilee in reality celebrated the union of England's greatest dramatist with England's finest actor, as reflected by Thomas Gainsborough's portrait commissioned for the new Town Hall depicting Garrick embracing the bust of Shakespeare in the Pembroke grounds at Wilton.

In conclusion, he writes: '[Garrick] drank from a Shakespeare-wood goblet and recited "As a relic I kiss it, and bow at the shrine. What comes from thy hand must be ever devine"'.[34] Thus the Shakespeare *memento mori* cottage industry evolved into a virtual canonisation in which relics were traded amongst advocates of the 'bard'.

Garrick has mulberry-based objects associated with his own life – a casket carved by Thomas Davies and made from mulberry wood and silver (*c.*1769) is in the collections of the British Museum. It contains low relief representations of Garrick, Shakespeare, King Lear and the Three Graces and was acquired in 1864 after it was bequeathed by George Daniel (Museum Number 1864-0816.1). This casket appears in a biography of Garrick, which gives a further perspective on the Shakespeare story when it states:

> Garrick, of course, knew that Shakespeare's mulberry tree was no more. In 1756 the steady trickle of visitors coming to Stratford had proved too troublesome to Reverend Francis Gastrell, the owner of Shakespeare's old home. He had annoyed the townsmen by having the tree felled at the dead of night … In 1762 Garrick himself bought some of the wood and had an elaborately carved chair made to Hogarth's design.[35]

William Hogarth (1697–1764), famous as a painter and illustrator, had a mulberry tree in his own garden at Chiswick (Survey List 3). A myth suggests that mulberry trees are able to protect against lightning; ironically, Hogarth's tree was apparently quite badly damaged by lightning during his lifetime. Garrick's chair has found its way into the Folger Shakespeare Library collections and is catalogued as the President's chair of the Shakespeare Club (Museum Number ART Inv. 1044), but is described as being intended for David Garrick's Temple to Shakespeare at Hampton. Importantly, the wood has been identified as mahogany and has no mulberry embellishments. This clearly highlights how the difference between fact and fiction can be very difficult to establish regarding Shakespeare's mulberry wood ephemera.

Into the twentieth century, Shakespeare-related items continued to sell in various auction houses in both this country and the USA. An article from 1905 in the *New York Times*, 'Shakespearean Relics Sell for High Prices', recorded the sale at Anderson Company of a mulberry wood tea caddy for $650 and other remotely connected items such as a G. Fisher model of Charlecote Hall – the seat of Sir Thomas Lucy (who Shakespeare ridiculed as Justice Shallow).[36] There is a mulberry tree at this site (Survey List 13). Christie's continues to sell Shakespeare items, including paper and wooden artefacts. A Christie's sale in 2011 had a selection of *memento mori* under the banner of Shakespeareana, including a mulberry goblet by John Marshall (1864) and a snuff box probably by the same maker (Illustration 82).[37] The company Thomas Coulborn & Sons advertised a beautiful small oval tea caddy for sale described as 'Shakespeare's mulberry wood made by Sharp of Stratford' (*c.*1780) which had decorative relief carving featuring mulberry imagery.[38] The Krone pen company have produced an expensive historic limited edition (388) Shakespeare fountain pen which contains some mulberry wood from Shakespeare's tree in the casing.

There are living mulberry trees associated with both Garrick and Shakespeare. The Shakespeare Birthplace Trust has a collection of mulberry trees (nine in total) in the grounds of the various houses in its care. Another old tree located in New Place featured in the *Stratford upon Avon Herald* in 1946 when it was badly damaged by a storm which meant the tree virtually collapsed.[39] The tree was said to have been planted in the exact position of the original Shakespeare mulberry and was thought to have come from a cutting from the original. The article states: 'The loss of the venerable tree, so much admired by pilgrims to Stratford-upon-Avon from all over the world, robs New Place and Nash's House for the time being of an outstanding beautiful and interesting feature.'[40] Another mulberry tree, identified by the Waymark code WM4A84, has a plaque which reads:

> The mulberry tree offspring
> of the parent tree nearby was
> planted by Dame Peggy Ashcroft
> on 8th September 1969 to com-
> memorate the 200th anniversary
> of the first Shakespeare Festival
> at Stratford-upon-Avon organised
> by David Garrick in 1769.

Yet another Garrick mulberry tree featured in *Classic Gardening Magazine*[41] when Andy Bull went in search of David Garrick's mulberry tree along Hampton Court Road in Surrey. He eventually located the tree (which he photographed) on land that would have been Garrick's back garden. It is often the case that mulberry trees are left stranded, as is also the case with the tree associated with John Evelyn detailed below. Finally, in *The Story of Silk* we read:

> There are probably numerous
> cuttings of Shakespeare's mul-
> berry tree which were carried all
> over England. A notable one is
> in Tamarisk Yard, Old Hastings
> where the famous Shakespearian
> actor David Garrick presented
> his friend Edward Capel (a noted
> Shakespearean scholar) with a
> cutting. That was in the 1770s.
> Now the large tree occupies most
> of the tiny courtyard, sheltered
> from the sea winds.[42]

Science, Symbols and Messages – Culpeper and Evelyn

As we have seen, herbals were an important source of information on plants and their uses in the Elizabethan period and beyond. They provided information on identity and usage whilst being used as a reference source for medics and herbalists. Perhaps the most famous is that by Nicholas Culpeper (1616–1654). *Culpeper's Complete Herbal* contains information on over 400 useful plants and herbs. Culpeper trained under Francis Drake who was an apothecary in Threadneedle Street, London and also gained knowledge from Thomas Johnson who edited the famous 1597 herbal by John Gerard. He eventually set up in practice as an apothecary in Red Lion Street in Spitalfields. In 1653, he published *The English Physician* (popularly known as *Culpeper's Complete Herbal*) and this has been in print ever since (see, for example, the facsimile edition produced in 2009 by Arcturus Publishing).[43] With regard to the mulberry tree he indicates that it bears fruit in July and August and states that it is so well known that it does not need to be illustrated. In a section entitled 'Government and Virtues', he writes:

> The mulberry partakes of differ-
> ent and opposite qualities; the
> ripe berries, by reason of their
> sweetness and slippery moisture,
> opening the body, and the unripe
> binding it, especially when they
> are dried; and then they are good
> to stay fluxes, lasks, and the
> abundance of women's menses.
> The bark of the root kills the
> broad worms in the body.

The mulberry tree has a variety of curative uses in oriental medicine and European research has investigated possible treatments for diabetes. Nicholas Culpeper is featured in Carolyn Fry's book *The Plant Hunters*[44] and the Wakehurst Place estate, which has a selection of mulberry trees, was once owned by a member of the Culpeper family.

John Evelyn (1620–1706) is perhaps best known for being a diarist, but he was also a gardener. He was educated at Balliol College, Oxford and the Middle Temple, London. He was a contemporary of both John Milton and Samuel Pepys (1633–1703). In 1652, Evelyn and his wife Mary Browne settled in Sayes Court in Deptford, London. The house was purchased from his father-in-law, Sir Richard Browne, and he acted upon his interest in trees and horticulture to create a large and impressive garden with over 300 fruit trees. The plans of this are archived in the British Library and can be viewed online in the John Evelyn archive under the title 'John Evelyn: Garden Theory, Garden Practice', where it states:

> The meticulous plan, provided
> with a key describing every
> feature, gives a unique and vivid
> evocation of the garden one con-
> temporary called 'the little world
> that goes under the name of
> Sayes Court.' It was first intended
> to communicate his ideas for the
> estate to his father-in-law, but
> the detailed nature of the plan
> suggests that Evelyn also had
> publication in mind.[45]

Remarkably, Mulberry Home produced a fabric (Illustration 6) which used very similar imagery to that in the John Evelyn drawings and plan. The garden, which was created from an orchard and pasture from 1652 to 1694, became famous, being viewed by various dignitaries including Peter the Great (1672–1725), who visited from Russia in January 1698. Indeed, the Minutes of the London County Council state that a black mulberry tree was thought to have been planted by Peter the Great (the 'Tsar of Muscovy', as Evelyn called him) during his visit: 'Mulberry Tree/Sayes Court, Greenwich is believed to have been planted by Peter the Great whilst a guest of the diarist John Evelyn was under some threat whilst the extension to the open space of Sayes Court took place.'[46] The matter was raised by a London County Council councillor Mrs Gollogly to the chairman of the Parks Committee during the meeting. After Evelyn's death the property had a chequered history and it was demolished in the 1720s with some of the salvaged material being used to build an almshouse, which was in turn demolished in 1930. Part of the grounds became a recreation area in 1878 and this was eventually eroded so that today the only evidence that exists of the actual garden of Sayes Court is a small and rather sad plot of land in Evelyn Street, with the mulberry tree remaining intact. Like so many mulberry trees it is the sole survivor in a landscape that has changed and evolved over time.

The longevity of mulberry trees is an advantage, alongside the feelings people have for these trees, which means that they are nearly always revered, preserved and protected. The Evelyn mulberry tree is mentioned in an article by Prudence Leith-Ross in *Garden History*.[47] This gives an extensive and detailed history of the garden and includes mention of the mulberry tree in relation to the island feature and moat. She writes: 'The island, to which a drawbridge over the moat gave access, was planted with "an hedge of severall fruits twixt 8 bedds of Asperge &c." Raspberries were planted at each end and there was a summer house in one corner and a mulberry tree at the eastern end.' This is shown on Joel Gascoyne's map and is annotated as Number 106 in the British Library plan.

John Evelyn is well known as an expert on trees and wrote the treatise *Sylva*,[48] first published in the early 1660s and made into many further editions in his lifetime. He makes mention of the black and white mulberry tree in *Dendrologia* Book II, 'of the mulberry':

> Morus, the mulberry: It may
> possibly be wondered by some
> why we should insert this tree
> amongst our forest inhabitants;
> but we shall soon reconcile our
> industrious planter when he
> comes to understand the incomparable benefit of it, and that

> for its timber, durableness, and
> use for the joiner and carpenter,
> and to make hoops, bows, wheels
> and even ribs for small vessels,
> instead of Oak etc., though the
> fruit and the leaves had not the
> due value with us, which they
> deservedly enjoy in other places
> of the world.

The discourse follows mulberry usage, propagation and various horticultural aspects of both black and white mulberry trees, making specific reference to silk cultivation. In addition, Evelyn gives guidance to prospective gardeners, including the following: 'That the first leaves putting forth of this wise tree (Sapientissima as Pliny calls it) is a more infallible note when those delicate plants may be safely brought out to air, than by any other prognostic or indication.' This is indeed true, and the mulberry tree (both black and white) is a very good indicator of spring, in that the leaves tend to open after the last severe frosts of winter.

Evelyn visited other gardens included in this study, including Squerryes Court (Survey List 37) in 1658 and Swallowfield Park (Survey List 57) in 1685, and in both cases he was enthusiastic about the environs and praised the landscape. His memory is extended by the American company Crabtree & Evelyn (founded 1972), which sell botanicals and fragrances from plant extracts such as Windsor Forest, and which in part is named after him, 'Crabtree' coming from the name for the wild apple or crab apple tree.[49]

Science, Symbols and Messages – Darwin and Hooker

Charles Darwin (1809–1882) was born to relative privilege and was educated at Christ's College, Cambridge, so he would have been familiar with Milton's mulberry in the Fellows' Garden. Darwin was interested in the natural sciences, and his mentor, Professor John Stevens Henslow, was influential in his further studies and lifelong interest in nature, including the collecting of beetles and herbarium specimens of plants. After considerable worldwide travel and life in London, he settled at Down House, Kent in 1842. When Darwin became resident, some of the mature trees were already in place, including an impressive horse chestnut (*Aesculus hippocastanum*) and the mulberry (*Morus nigra*) along with yew (*Taxus baccata*) and Scots pine (*Pinus sylvestris*). The house became a home for his family, including eight children, and an extensive family tree features in the guidebook *Charles Darwin at Down House*, which is an English Heritage publication.[50] In her book, Pilgrimage, the photographer Annie Liebovitz writes about Darwin after a visit to the United Kingdom:

> Down House became the centre of Darwin's world. He rarely left it. He doubled the size of the original house, built a greenhouse, and cultivated extensive gardens. His daily routine included two or three walks on a looping path, the Sandwalk, that he had planted with trees and bushes. It was where he spent time thinking before going back to his study.[51]

During this pilgrimage Liebovitz visited many famous sites attached to significant people, including Monticello, Sissinghurst and Down House. The mulberry tree at Down (Survey List 14) is located outside the nursery and was fondly remembered by Charles Darwin's children and grandchildren. The black mulberry tree is pictured near to the nursery window in her book, *Period Piece: A Cambridge Childhood*,[52] by artist Gwen Raverat (1885–1957), the daughter of Charles Darwin's son George (1845–1912). The English Heritage guidebook, *Charles Darwin at Down House*, declares: 'In her book *Period Piece* (1952), Raverat describes the special atmosphere of Down and the happy times spent there. She felt that the Darwin family was so close that, as adults, the children found it difficult to move away and be independent.'

The house was a base for Charles Darwin during his most productive years, including the publication of *On the Origin of Species* in 1859. In his conclusion, Darwin writes:

> It is interesting to contemplate a tangled bank, clothed with many plants of many kinds, with birds singing in the bushes, with various insects flitting about, and with worms crawling through the damp earth, and to reflect that these elaborately constructed forms, so different from each other, and dependent upon each other in so complex a manner, have all been produced by laws acting around us.[53]

The house is now in the care of English Heritage and is open for visitors after an extensive restoration project of both the house and garden – the black mulberry tree being central to their plans. Darwin's portrait has also featured on the Bank of England's £10 note.

The most beautiful recording of the black mulberry and the object prized above all others is the botanical illustration by William Hooker (1779–1832), who was known as both an artist and an engraver.[54] He was the finest fruit illustrator of his generation and will probably be regarded as the greatest exponent of fruit depiction that has ever lived. His illustrations are refined and exquisite in detail and are extremely accurate. This is probably due to his background and his interest in botany alongside his undoubted skill in draughtsmanship. Not a great deal is known about his life but it is certain that he became a pupil of Francis Bauer (1758–1840) who was the official botanical artist at Kew. In *The Collector's Portfolio of Hooker's Fruits*, it says of Bauer:

> Bauer's most famous work was *Delineations of Exotic Plants Cultivated in the Royal Gardens at Kew* (1796). The very accurate, detailed plates were judged so precise as not to require an accompanying textual description. His precision, skilful technique and elegant presentation must have been a profoundly formative influence upon the young Hooker.[55]

In *Hooker's Finest Fruits*, it states: 'Indeed Hooker's fruit paintings may be regarded as pomological counterparts of Bauer's botanical ones; they display the same quality of life-like precise representation.'[56] After some collaborative work William Hooker started to produce illustrations on his own, including 117 plates for Richard Anthony Salisbury's (1791–1829) *Paradisus Londinensis*, which was finished in 1809. In addition, he produced illustrative work for Thomas Andrew Knight's (1759–1838) *Pomona Herefordiensis* (old cider and perry fruits), from 1808 to 1811, and Frederick Purse's (1774–1826) *Flora Americae Septentrionalis*, published in 1814. He was for much of his adult life associated with the London Horticultural Society (which later became the Royal Horticultural Society) and was elected to the Fruit Committee, and he made 158 illustrations for the fruit illustration collection between 1815 and 1821. These are now housed in the Lindley Library at the Royal Horticultural Society. Between 1813 and 1818, he produced what is considered to be his finest work – *Pomona Londinensis*, which illustrated English garden fruits.

After this time ill health meant that his artistic career ceased and he died in London in 1832. The black mulberry branch produced by

William Hooker in 1816 is shown in Illustration 83. Sadly (and possibly a misjudgement by the RHS), the Hooker mulberry illustration appears on scented drawer liners and other giftware produced by Wax Lyrical,[57] which has the seal of approval of the Royal Horticultural Society. It states on the packaging:

> This classic illustration of the Black Mulberry, taken from the world renowned RHS Lindley Library in London, is the inspiration for the fragrance of 'Mulberry'. Created by expert perfumers, the rich fragrance depicts the aroma of sun ripened plump mulberries, picked fresh from the tree.

Alas, the fragrance has a sickly and cheap smell and the Hooker illustration deserves better – it should never have been used on such products, particularly in the awful montage style. In far better taste, a contemporary project, instigated by HRH Prince Charles, has resurrected the tradition of using botanical illustrations to record a plant collection, the *Highgrove Florilegium*. The flora was produced in 2008/2009 from a series of contemporary illustrations of plants and trees located at his home and on the estate of the Prince of Wales at Highgrove; it was produced in a limited edition of 175 sets of two volumes, which retail at £12,950. A letter from Highgrove in 2012 indicates that the garden contains mulberry trees, but the publisher, Addison Publications, confirms that they do not feature in the *Highgrove Florilegium*.[58]

A series of pamphlets entitled 'The Great Poets'[59] was produced by the *Independent* newspaper in 2008 and contained summary information on some of the poets who have been featured in this study, including Shakespeare, Milton and Keats. John Keats's house, with its black mulberry tree, is featured as Survey List 80. Further literary associations can be found at Renishaw Hall (Survey List 77), the home of the writer Edith Sitwell (1887–1964). Other associations have not been photographically recorded in the study but include a mulberry tree planted by William Wordsworth (1770–1850) in 1845, located in the grounds of Wray Castle on the banks of Lake Windermere, Cumbria.[60] Rudyard Kipling (1865–1936) also had a mulberry garden at his house Bateman's and it is known that he planted a mulberry tree in 1905 but it died in the 1960s (see the Bateman's National Trust guidebook for the plan of the garden). A lineage of writers and poets has been established who have specific connections with black mulberry trees. It is likely that some of these trees have significance because of the Shakespeare connection and the undoubted reputation he has amongst those who write.

In *American Material Culture* it states: 'Carefully organized observation of, and research about, objects has long been the foundation of Winterthur's interpretation.'[61] The Watson box in the collections of Winterthur was really the inspiration that started this study because of the connections made between the objects found in the box and the various woods that the items were made from. Under normal circumstances wood is not considered a valuable material (unlike gold or silver). However, added value is achieved by the fact that the woods have associations with trees that were planted and owned by significant and often honoured people. There is no better example of this than that of the mulberry wood associated with Shakespeare. The layers of meaning of these objects create layers of value which may not necessarily always equate to amounts of money. However, in the case of Shakespeare it is in a purely non-cynical way that value and price are connected.

Conclusion

Material culture is mainly concerned with observation and interpretation. A variety of publications from the Winterthur Museum have emphasised the role that the eye has in the interpretation of objects, from *Seeing Things Differently*[62] to *Eye for Excellence: Masterworks from Winterthur*.[63] Objects should be analysed by sight and then by other means, including touch. The advantage of this study is that nearly all the objects have been photographed directly and the mulberry trees recorded *in situ*. The form and mood of the objects can be assessed and style considerations interpreted particularly in the case of the contrast between United Kingdom- and Japanese-made objects. The study has highlighted the type and range of objects associated with mulberry trees in two- and three-dimensional forms. It has also endeavoured to place these within a social and economic context whilst highlighting usage, such as in the tea ceremony. It has also analysed the connections with people that in the end are so important. Nearly all the objects featured in the study can be used and have a function which is associated with both their form and context. In the recent BBC Radio 4 series *Searching for Shakespeare*, context referenced via material culture methods was documented.[64] Taking the sight and touch aspect further, this included a relic in the collections of Stoneyhurst College,

Lancashire. Neil MacGregor writes:

> I'm holding in the palm of my
> hand what looks a bit like a small
> circular box of mints. But the
> inscription on it is not for sugar-
> free peppermints. It is four short
> lines of Latin. When I turn the
> box over, I can see a window that
> shows what's inside. The window
> is in the shape of an eye.

In fact, the box with eyelash embellishments contains the right eyeball of Edward Oldcorne – a reliquary or *memento mori* from *c*.1606. It is an eye that cannot see but it provides an insight into the world which William Shakespeare inhabited and thus makes his world more understandable in the contemporary context.

It is here that the final statement comes in the form of a quotation taken from the book by Edmund de Waal, *The Hare with Amber Eyes*. He is speaking of a netsuke that he carries around in his pocket:

> This was a netsuke of a very ripe
> medlar fruit, made out of chest-
> nut wood in the late eighteenth
> century in Edo, the old Tokyo. In
> autumn in Japan you sometimes
> see medlars; a branch hanging
> over the wall of a temple ... My
> medlar is just about to go from
> ripeness to deliquescence. The
> three leaves at the top feel as
> if they would fall if you rubbed
> them between your fingers. The
> fruit is slightly unbalanced: it is
> riper on one side than the other.
> Underneath, you can feel the
> two holes – one larger than the
> other – where the silk would run,
> so that the netsuke could act as
> a toggle on a small bag. I try and
> imagine who owned the medlar.[65]

Edmund de Waal talks about a hidden inheritance: I hope that the hidden material culture of the mulberry tree has now been made visible.

Notes to Chapter 5

1   Graves, *Seeing Things Differently*, p. 68.
2   For details of the poem that was written to commemorate the planting of a slip of Milton's mulberry tree at Woburn Abbey and an illustration of the pressed mulberry leaf, see Milton Keynes Heritage Association website: www.mkheritage.co.uk/wsc/docs/wiffenbrothers.html ('The Literary Wiffen Brothers') (accessed 25 November 2012). See also Diana Wells, *Lives of the Trees: An Uncommon History* (New York: Algonquin Books, 2010). The mulberry tree is featured on pp. 215–218 with details of the story of Pyramus and Thisbe and reference to Shakespeare.
3   See www.allenhall.org.uk. There was also a series of documentaries broadcast on BBC4 television in 2012, *Priests to Be: Inside Allen Hall Seminary, Westminster*, directed by Richard Alwyn.
4   See www.angelalorenzartistsbooks.com, with specific reference to *The Strength of Denham* by Angela Lorenz: www.angelalorenzartistsbooks.com/opere/denham.htm (accessed 12 December 2012).
5   William Roper, *The Life of Sir Thomas More*, www.forgottenbooks.org, first published *c*.1626 (during his lifetime). The lives of saints are featured on a website, www.catholic.org/saints. The website indicates that the feast day of Saint Thomas More is 22 June and that he is the patron saint of lawyers.
6   'Milton's Mulberry', episode 5 (of 8), of *Meetings with Remarkable Trees*, BBC4 television programme. See Chapter 1 n. 8, above.
7   On 15 June 2010, the Post Office produced a series of themed stamps on the Tudors and Stuarts. The 88p stamp illustrated a portrait of John Milton (from the National Portrait Gallery), to celebrate the publication of *Paradise Lost* in 1667. The stamp featured in The Age of the Stuarts, Kings and Queens sheet of stamps, with an attached timeline designed by Atelier Works. See www.bfdc.co.uk/2010/miniature_sheets/.
8   Charles Lesingham Smith, 'Milton's Mulberry Tree', in *The Cambridge Portfolio*, vol. 1 (Cambridge: Cambridge University Press, 2009 [1840]), p. 207.
9   'Milton's Mulberry', *Meetings with Remarkable Trees*, BBC4 television programme.
10 John Blatchly, 'Milton and the Mulberry Tree', *East Anglian Daily Times*, 28 June 2008, p. 24.
11 'Milton's Mulberry', *Meetings with Remarkable Trees*, BBC4 television programme.
12 See www.bmagic.org.uk (accessed 26 August 2012).
13 Michael Parry, *Morris & Co.: A Revolution in Decoration* (Denham: Morris & Co., 2011), pp. 56 and 57.
14 Ibid., p. 18.
15 See Kathy Haslam, *William Morris: A Sense of Place*, with a foreword by Adam Naylor (Bowness-on-Windermere: Lakeland Arts Trust, 2010). Produced as part of the exhibition held at Blackwell, The Arts and Crafts House, 26 June–17 October 2010.
16 William Morris, *Poems By The Way* (London: Kelmscott Press, 1891).
17 Available at www.gutenberg.org/ebooks/3468 (accessed 12 December 2012).
18 Crossley, Hassall and Salway, *William Morris's Kelmscott Landscape and History*, p. 5.
19 Fiona MacCarthy, *William Morris: A Life for Our Time* (London: Faber and Faber, 2010).
20 A. R. Dufty, *Kelmscott Manor: An Illustrated Guide*, revised by John Cherry (London: Society of Antiquaries of London, 2004). The garden is featured on pp. 38–39.
21 Ibid., p. 39

22 Alastair Sooke, 'William Morris Gallery Re-opening, Lloyd Park, London – Review', *Daily Telegraph*, 1 August 2012, www.telegraph.co.uk/culture/art/art-reviews/9441970/William-Morris-Gallery-re-opening-Lloyd-Park-London-review.html (accessed 16 December 2012).

23 www.factum-arte.com/pag/107/The--span-Walthamstow-Tapestry--span- (accessed 16 December 2012).

24 *Fakes, Forgeries & Facsimiles*, The Folger Shakespeare Library, 20 August 2003–3 January 2004, http://folgerpedia.folger.edu/Fakes,_Forgeries_%26_Facsimiles.

25 *The Centenary Letters by William Cowper*, with an introduction by Simon Malpas (Manchester: Carcanet Press, 2000).

26 See www.mkheritage.co.uk/www.cowperandnewton-museum.org.uk (accessed 30 December 2012).

27 Letter dated 19 September 2012 from K. Mumford of Wilkin & Sons (Tiptree), who gives the quotation by William Cowper as 'Variety is the very spice of life, that gives it all of its flavour'. The letter indicates that the advertisements were screened during the ITV television series *Tasty Travels* presented by Linda Bellingham.

28 See http://janus.lib.cam.ac.uk/db/node.xsp?id=EAD%2FGBR%2F0271%2FGCPP%20Gamble (accessed 6 January 2013).

29 See Tarnya Cooper, *Searching for Shakespeare*, with essays by Marcia Pointon, James Shapiro and Stanley Wells (London: National Portrait Gallery Publications, 2006), p. 143. The catalogue was produced to accompany the exhibition at the National Portrait Gallery, 2 March–29 May 2006.

30 Janel Jacobson, *Ark of the Founders* (2010). This featured in an exhibition called *National Treasures* that was curated by William Jewell of Historical Woods of America, http://ohiocraft.org/ocm-exhibitions/past/2011-2/national-treasures/jacobsentrayfull-2/.

31 *Important English Furniture*, a sale held at Sotheby's, London, 29 November 2000. The quotation is taken from the annotation to Lot 1: 'A Rare George II Tea Caddy circa 1759 by George Cooper', which realised £12,000. Information received from Jeremy Smith (English Furniture Department) at Sotheby's in a letter dated 4 October 2007. This caddy appears in Bowett, *Woods in British Furniture Making, 1400–1900*, p. 159 (M55).

32 John Hardy, 'Ryland's "Shakespeare Wood" Tea Caddy', *Christie's International Magazine*, June–July 1990, p. 80.

33 Robert Bleasdale, 'Shakespeare's Mulberry Tree', *Antique Collecting: The Journal of the Antique Collector's Club*, 47.6 (2012) (The Art Issue), pp. 32–37.

34 Hardy, 'Ryland's "Shakespeare Wood" Tea Caddy'.

35 See Helen R. Smith, *David Garrick, 1717–1779, A Brief Account*, British Library Monograph 1 (London: British Library, 1979), pp. 24–30. The caddy is illustrated on p. 25.

36 'Shakespearean Relics Sell for High Prices', *New York Times*, 3 November 1905. In the archives of the Folger Shakespeare Library, Washington, DC.

37 *Fine Printed Books and Manuscripts*, a sale held at Christie's, London, 13 June 2011: Shakespeariana featuring in Lots 85–89 (pp. 30–31).

38 An email communication dated 12 October 2012 from Jonathan Coulborn indicated that the caddy was probably first owned by Robert Graham of Gartmore House, Stirling, Scotland. The Cunninghame-Graham family had connections with the USA and apparently exported mulberry trees to Virginia in the eighteenth century.

39 'After the Storm: New Place Mulberry Tree Crashes', with a photograph by Thos. F. Holte, *Stratford upon Avon Herald*, 16 August 1946. In the archives of the Folger Shakespeare Library, Washington, DC.

40 The newspaper cutting is located in the Archive of the Shakespeare Birthplace Trust (DR357/1/1).

41 www.classicgardeningmagazine.co.uk (accessed 2 March 2012); no longer available.

42 Feltwell, *The Story of Silk*, p. 108.

43 Nicholas Culpeper, *Culpeper's Complete Herbal*, with an introduction by Diana Vowles (London: Arcturus Publishing, 2009). This is based on the original printing, *The English Physician*, which was finished in 1653.

44 Carolyn Fry, *The Plant Hunters: The Adventures of the World's Greatest Botanical Explorers* (London: Carlton Publishing Group, 2009).

45 See www.bl.uk/onlinegallery/onlineex/deptford/s/008add000016945u00071000.html (accessed 24 August 2012).

46 Minutes of the London County Council (1951), p. 49. Located in the London Metropolitan Archives (part of the National Archives, Kew).

47 Prudence Leith-Ross, 'The Garden of John Evelyn at Deptford', *Garden History*, 25.2 (1997), pp. 138–152.

48 Both a facsimile copy and a modern reprint of the mulberry section from *Sylva* are located in the Titchmarsh & Goodwin archive. There is a new, contemporary, '*Sylva*', 'taking inspiration from the original work': see Gabriel Hemery and Sarah Simblet, *The New Sylva: A Discourse of Forest and Orchard Trees for the Twenty-first Century* (London: Bloomsbury, 2014).

49 The Crabtree & Evelyn website features an illustration of both John Evelyn and the crab apple tree. It also claims that John Evelyn's personal motto was 'Explore everything. Keep the best.' www.crabtree-evelyn.co.uk/about-us/history/ (accessed 2 November 2012).

50 Solene Morris, Louise Wilson and David Kohn, *Charles Darwin at Down House* (London: English Heritage, 2006), with specific reference to the gatefold on the last page.

51 Annie Liebovitz, *Pilgrimage* (London: Jonathan Cape, 2011), p. 36.

52 Gwen Raverat, *Period Piece: A Cambridge Childhood* (London: Faber and Faber, 1952). The illustration can be found on p. 143 in the chapter 'Down'. There are family trees on pp. 12 and 13.

53 Morris, Wilson and Kohn, *Charles Darwin at Down House*, p. 60.

54 William Hooker should not be confused with his namesake William Jackson Hooker (1785–1865), who was also an illustrator, and chair of Botany at Glasgow University and later the director at Kew.

55 Jean Marriott, *The Collector's Portfolio of Hooker's Fruits* (London: Aurum Press, in association with Swallow Publishing, 1989), p. 2.

56 William T. Stearn and Frederick A. Roach, *Hooker's Finest Fruits: A Selection of Paintings of Fruits by William Hooker (1779–1832)* (London: Prentice Hall, 1989), p. 12.

57 Wax Lyrical produced a series of scented products including candles, potpourris and drawer liners in collaboration with the Royal Horticultural Society, which granted the manufacturing licence in 2009.

58 Letter correspondence dated 21 August 2012 to the

author from Debs Goodenough (Head Gardener to the Prince of Wales and the Duchess of Cornwall), Highgrove, Gloucestershire. Plus a telephone conversation with Addison Publications Ltd on 24 August 2012. In addition, a small brochure was sent dated 25 August detailing the project and context.

59 Michael Schmidt, 'The Great Poets', *Independent* (2008). The series was accompanied by a CD and featured 14 poets, including booklets on Shakespeare (no. 2), Milton (no. 4), Wordsworth (no. 8) and Keats (no. 9).

60 Letter correspondence dated 9 April 2008 to the author from the Wordsworth Trust.

61 Ann Smart Martin and J. Ritchie Garrison (eds), *American Material Culture: The Shape of the Field* (Winterthur, Del.: Henry Francis du Pont Winterthur Museum, 1997), p. 140.

62 Graves, *Seeing Things Differently*.

63 Donald L. Fennimore and staff at Winterthur, *Eye for Excellence: Masterworks from Winterthur* (Winterthur,

Del.: Winterthur Museum and Gardens, 1994).

64 *Shakespeare's Restless World*, BBC Radio 4 series, written and presented by Neil MacGregor, first broadcast in a series of 20 programmes in 2012, www.bbc.co.uk/programmes/b01h7cdr. The series was a partnership between Radio 4 and the British Museum. Repackaged in a CD box set, with illustrated booklet (BBC Audiobooks Ltd., 2011). An associated exhibition called *Shakespeare: Staging the World* was held at the British Museum, 19 July–25 November 2012.

65 Edmund de Waal, *The Hare with Amber Eyes: A Hidden Inheritance* (London: Chatto & Windus, 2010), p. 12. The medlar is illustrated in Edmund de Waal, *The Hare with Amber Eyes: The Illustrated Edition* (London: Chatto & Windus, 2011). The illustration is part of the endpapers (on the bottom shelf) with annotation on p. 410. He further discussed this with Kirsty Young on *Desert Island Discs* on BBC Radio 4, first broadcast in 2012; www.bbc.co.uk/programmes/b01p067p.

84 English Georgian eye
'mulberry' snuffbox

Bibliography

Altshuler, Bruce, *Isamu Noguchi (Modern Masters)* (New York: Abbeville Press, 1995).

Aslet, Clive, 'Are the Streets Still Paved with Gold?', *Country Life*, 12–19 December 2012, pp. 128–132.

Barriault, Anne B., and Kay M. Davidson, *The Virginia Museum of Fine Arts* (Charlottesville, Va.: University of Virginia Press, 2007).

Bazeley, Bonham, 'Royal Mulberries', *Garden*, June 1992, pp. 284–286.

Blackburne-Maze, Peter, *Fruit: An Illustrated History* (London: Scriptum Editions, in association with the Royal Horticultural Society, 2003).

Bleasdale, Robert, 'Shakespeare's Mulberry Tree', *Antique Collecting: The Journal of the Antique Collector's Club*, 47.6 (2012) (The Art Issue), pp. 32–37.

Bowe, Stephen, 'A Rare Japanese Mulberry Wood Called Shimakuwa', *Woodland Heritage* (2009), pp. 24–25.

Bowett, Adam, *Early Georgian Furniture, 1715–1740* (Woodbridge: The Antique Collectors' Club, 2009).

–– *English Furniture, 1660–1714, from Charles II to Queen Anne* (Woodbridge: The Antique Collectors' Club, 2002).

–– 'Furniture Woods in London and Provincial Furniture, 1700–1800', *Regional Furniture Journal*, 22 (2008), pp. 87–113.

–– 'Stained Burr Maple v. Burr Mulberry: A Final Word' (with a short reply by Peter Goodwin), *Woodland Heritage* (2008), pp. 62–63.

–– *Woods in British Furniture Making, 1400–1900 (An Illustrated Historical Dictionary)* (Wetherby: Oblong Creative Ltd, 2012).

Boyer, Marie-France, 'Japan in Soft Focus', *World of Interiors*, 31.6 (2011), pp. 136–145.

The British Museum Souvenir Guide (London: British Museum Press, 2009).

Burford, Beverley, *Images of Charlton House: A Pictorial History* (London: Greenwich Council, 2002).

Burks, Jean M., *Shaker Design: Out of this World* (New Haven, Conn.: Yale University Press, 2008).

Burroughs, Katrina, 'One Good Turn', *BBC Homes and Antiques*, March 2006, pp. 43–49.

Bushell, Raymond, *Inro Handbook* (Tokyo: Weatherhill Inc., 1990).

Butler, Maureen, *Gordon Russell: Vision and Reality* (Broadway: Gordon Russell Museum, 2007).

Caldicott, Chris, 'Discover – The Gardens of Japan', *Homes & Gardens*, May 2012, pp. 201–204.

Calza, Gian Carlo, *Japan Style* (London: Phaidon Press, 2007).

Capell, Kerry, 'Ikea's New Plan for Japan', *Business Week*, 25 April 2006, www.bloomberg.com/bw/stories/2006-04-25/ikeas-new-plan-for-japan.

Chapin, Helen B., 'Themes of the Japanese Netsuke Carver', *The Art Bulletin: An Illustrated Quarterly*, 5.1 (1922) (The College Art Association of America), pp. 10–21.

Coleno, Nadine, *The Hermès Scarf: History and Mystique* (London: Thames & Hudson, 2009).

Cooper, Tarnya, *Searching for Shakespeare*, with essays by Marcia Pointon, James Shapiro and Stanley Wells (London: National Portrait Gallery Publications, 2006).

Cowper, William, *The Centenary Letters by William Cowper*, with an introduction by Simon Malpas (Manchester: Carcanet Press, 2000).

Crossley, Alan, Tom Hassall and Peter Salway (eds), *William Morris's Kelmscott Landscape and History* (Macclesfield: Windgather Press, 2007).

Culpeper, Nicholas, *Culpeper's Complete Herbal*, with an introduction by Diana Vowles (London: Arcturus Publishing, 2009).

'Current and Forthcoming Exhibitions', *Burlington Magazine*, 118.884 (1976), pp. 785–787.

David Linley Gifts and Accessories Catalogue, 2011–2012 (London: David Linley, 2011).

de Waal, Edmund, *The Hare with Amber Eyes: A Hidden Inheritance* (London: Chatto & Windus, 2010).

–– *The Hare with Amber Eyes: The Illustrated Edition* (London: Chatto & Windus, 2011).

Deep Rooted: How Trees Shape Our Lives, exhibition pamphlet (Manchester: Whitworth Art Gallery, 2010).

Dennison, Matthew, 'Paper Trail', *World of Interiors*, 28.7 (2008), pp. 68–77.

Desmond, Steven, 'On a Cold and Frosty Morning', with photographs by Allan Pollok-Morris, *Country Life*, 12–19 December 2012, pp. 88–93.

Don, Monty, *Around the World in 80 Gardens* (London: Weidenfeld & Nicolson, 2008).

Dufty, A. R., *Kelmscott Manor: An Illustrated Guide*, revised by John Cherry (London: Society of Antiquaries of London, 2004).

Duncan, R. S., *The West Riding House of Correction and H.M. Prison Wakefield* (Wakefield: Wakefield Print & Design, 1995).

Evans, Sian, *To the Manor Reborn: The Transformation of Avebury Manor* (London: National Trust Books, 2011).

Faulkner, Rupert, *Japanese Studio Crafts Tradition and the Avant-Garde* (London: Laurence King, 1995).

Feltwell, John, *The Story of Silk* (Stroud: Alan Sutton Publishing, 1990).

Fendley, Georgia (ed.), *Mulberry: Est. 1971* (Bath: Mulberry Company (Design) Limited, 2011).

Fennimore, Donald L., and staff at Winterthur, *Eye for Excellence: Masterworks from Winterthur* (Winterthur, Del.: Winterthur Museum and Gardens, 1994).

Fischer, Felice (ed.), *The Art of Japanese Craft: 1875 to Present* (New Haven, Conn.: Philadelphia Museum of Art, in association with Yale University Press, 2008).

FitzHerbert, Richard, *Tissington Hall Guidebook* (Derby: Derbyshire Countryside Ltd, 2003).

Foister, Susan, Ashok Roy and Martin Wyld, *Making and Meaning: Holbein's Ambassadors, An Exhibition Catalogue* (London: National Gallery Publications, 1997).

Foulkes, Nick, and Charles March, *Dunhill by Design: A Very English Story* (Paris: Flammarion, 2006).

Fry, Carolyn, *The Plant Hunters: The Adventures of the World's Greatest Botanical Explorers* (London: Carlton Publishing Group, 2009).

Gaddum, A. H., *Silk: How and Where it is Produced* (Macclesfield: H. T. Gaddum & Company, 1989).

Girouard, Mark, 'The Derbyshire Dowagers', *World of Interiors*, 28.11 (2008), pp. 120–131.

Goodwin, Peter, 'Mulberry Burr versus Stained Burr Maple', *Woodland Heritage* (2006), pp. 38–39.

–– 'Mulberry Burr versus Stained Burr Maple: The Debate Continues', *Woodland Heritage* (2007), p. 13.

Gordon, Catherine, *Chipping Campden (Towns and Villages of England)* (Stroud: Alan Sutton Publishing, 1993).

Goudge, Elizabeth, *The Joy of the Snow* (New York: Coward, McCann & Geoghegan, 1974).

Graves, Thomas A. (ed.), *Seeing Things Differently: An Exhibition Catalogue* (Little Compton, RI: Winterthur Publications and Fort Church Publishers, 1992).

Greenacre, Francis, and Stephen Ponder, *Tyntesfield Guidebook* (London: National Trust, 2005).

Hardy, John, 'Ryland's "Shakespeare Wood" Tea Caddy', *Christie's International Magazine*, June–July 1990, p. 80.

Haslam, Kathy, *William Morris: A Sense of Place*, with a foreword by Adam Naylor (Bowness-on-Windermere: Lakeland Arts Trust, 2010).

Heal, Ambrose (Sir), *The London Furniture Makers: From the Restoration to the Victorian Era, 1660–1840* (New York: Dover Publications, 1953).

Hudson's Historic Houses and Gardens, Castles and Heritage Sites (Banbury: Norman Hudson & Co., 2003).

Humery, Gabriel, and Sarah Simblet, *The New Sylva: A Discourse of Forest and Orchard Trees for the Twenty-first Century* (London: Bloomsbury, 2014).

Hunting, Penelope, *A History of The Drapers' Company* (London: Drapers' Company, 1989).

Hussey, Christopher, 'Eltham Hall', *Country Life*, 15 May 1937, pp. 534–539; 22 May 1937, pp. 568–573; 29 May 1937, pp. 594–599.

Hutt, Julia, *Japanese Netsuke*, with a foreword by Edmund de Waal (London: V&A Publications, 2012).

Jackson, Anna, *The V&A Guide to Period Styles: 400 Years of British Art and Design* (London: V&A Publications, 2006).

Jacobson, Dawn, *Chinoiserie* (London: Phaidon Press, 1993).

The Japanese Craft Tradition: Kokten Korgei, with a foreword by Edward King and an essay by Professor Samiro Yunoki (Bowness-on-Windermere: Lakeland Arts Trust, 2001).

Japanese Crafts: A Complete Guide to Today's Traditional Handmade Objects, with an introduction by Diane Durston (Tokyo: Kodansha International, 1996).

Kakuzo, Okakura, *The Book of Tea*, with an afterword by Jim Massey (Philadelphia, Pa.: Running Press, 2002).

Kenji, Kaneko, 'The Development of "Traditional Crafts" in Japan', in Nicole Rousmaniere (ed.), *Crafting Beauty in Modern Japan* (London: British Museum Press, 2007).

Kichiemon, Okamura, *Japanese Ikat* (Kyoto: Fujioka Mamoru, Kyoto Shoin Co., 1993).

Kindred Spirits: The Eloquence of Function in American Shaker and Japanese Arts of Daily Life, with a foreword by Martha W. Longenecker (San Diego, Calif.: Mingei International Museum, 1995).

Kiritani, Elizabeth, *Vanishing Japan: Traditions, Crafts and Culture* (Tokyo: Tuttle Publishing, 1995).

Koidzumi, G., 'Taxonomy and Phytogeography of the Genus *Morus*', *Bulletin of Sericultural Experimental Station* (Tokyo), 3 (1917), pp. 1–62.

Koizumi, Kazuko, *Traditional Japanese Furniture: A Definitive Guide*, translated by Alfred Birnbaum (Tokyo: Kodansha International, 1986).

Kyoko, Tsukada, 'We Have Nurtured Trees since Time Immemorial to Get the Precious Drops', *Kateigaho International*, winter edition (2007), p. 39.

Leith-Ross, Prudence, 'The Garden of John Evelyn at Deptford', *Garden History*, 25.2 (1997), pp. 138–152.

Liebovitz, Annie, *Pilgrimage* (London: Jonathan Cape, 2011).

Linford, Jenny, *A Concise Guide to Trees* (Bicester: Baker and Taylor, 2009).

Mabey, Richard, *Beechcombings: A Narrative of Trees* (London: Chatto & Windus, 2007).

MacCarthy, Fiona, *William Morris: A Life for Our Time* (London: Faber and Faber, 2010).

MacGregor, Neil, *A History of the World in 100 Objects* (London: Allen Lane, 2010).

Macquoid, Percy, and Ralph Edwards, *The Dictionary of English Furniture*, 3 vols (Woodbridge: The Antique Collectors' Club, 1983 [1954]).

Mair, Victor H., and Erling Hoh, *The True History of Tea* (London: Thames & Hudson, 2009).

Marriott, Jean, *The Collector's Portfolio of Hooker's Fruits* (London: Aurum Press, in association with Swallow Publishing, 1989).

Martin, Ann Smart, and J. Ritchie Garrison (eds), *American Material Culture: The Shape of the Field* (Winterthur, Del.: Henry Francis du Pont Winterthur Museum, 1997).

Meijer, Fred G., *Dutch and Flemish Still-Life Paintings* (Amsterdam: Waanders Publishers, in collaboration with the Ashmolean Museum, Oxford, 2003).

The More-Molyneux family, *Loseley Park Guidebook* (Derby: Heritage House Group Ltd, 1994).

Morrall, Andrew, and Melinda Watt (eds), *English Embroidery from the Metropolitan Museum of Art, 1580–1700: Twixt Art and Nature. An Exhibition Catalogue* (New York: Bard Graduate Center for Studies in the Decorative Arts, Design and Culture, 2008).

Morris, Solene, Louise Wilson and David Kohn, *Charles Darwin at Down House* (London: English Heritage, 2006).

Morris, William, *Poems By The Way* (London: Kelmscott Press, 1891).

Nichols, Frederick D., and James A. Bear, Jr, *Monticello: A Guidebook* (Charlottesville, Va.: Thomas Jefferson Memorial Foundation, 1993).

Nishikawa, Takaaki, *Nihon no mori to ki no Shokunin* [Forests in Japan and Craftsmen of Wood] (Tokyo: Diamond Big Co., 2007).

Ohki, Sadako, *Tea Culture of Japan*, with a contribution by Takeshi Watanabe (New Haven, Conn.: Yale University Art Gallery, 2009).

Pakenham, Thomas, *Meetings with Remarkable Trees* (London: Weidenfeld & Nicolson, 1996).

Parry, Michael, *Morris & Co.: A Revolution in Decoration* (Denham: Morris & Co., 2011).

Pavey, Ruth, 'Sources of Inspiration: Mary Restieaux', *Crafts* (July–August 2002), pp. 37–39.

Peers, Simon, *Golden Spider Silk* (London: V&A Publications, 2012).

Pinto, Edward H., 'The Myth of the Mulberry Burr Veneer', *Country Life*, 2 October 1969, pp. 794–795.

–– *Treen and Other Wooden Bygones: An Encyclopaedia and Social History* (London: G. Bell & Sons, 1969).

Pitelka, Morgan, *Japanese Tea Culture: Art, History and Practice* (London: Routledge, 2003).

Pospielovsky, Juliet, 'A Serving of Tradition', *BBC Homes and Antiques*, January 2007, pp. 84–89.

Prown, Jules David, 'Mind in Matter: An Introduction to Material Culture Theory and Method', *Winterthur Portfolio*, 17.1 (1982), pp. 1–19.

Raverat, Gwen, *Period Piece: A Cambridge Childhood* (London: Faber and Faber, 1952).

Rousmaniere, Nicole (ed.), *Crafting Beauty in Modern Japan* (London: British Museum Press, 2007).

Russell, Jesse, and Ronald Cohn, *Izu Islands* (Edinburgh: Bookvika Publishing, 2012).

Sackville-West, Robert, *Knole Guidebook* (Swindon: National Trust, 1998).

Saito, Jun, *Tokyo no shima* [Islands of Tokyo] (Tokyo: Kobunsha, 2007).

Sample, Geoff, *Garden Bird Songs and Calls* (London: HarperCollins Publishers, 2000).

Sargeant, Diane, 'A Secret History of Taste: Gainsborough Silk Mill', *Journal for Weavers, Spinners and Dyers*, 239 (2011), pp. 24–27.

Saul, Roger, *Mulberry at Home* (London: Ebury Press, 1999).

Schoeser, Mary, *Silk* (New Haven, Conn.: Yale University Press, 2007).

Smith, Charles Lesingham, 'Milton's Mulberry Tree', *The Cambridge Portfolio*, vol. 1 (Cambridge: Cambridge University Press, 2009 [1840]).

Smith, Helen R., *David Garrick, 1717–1779, A Brief Account*, British Library Monograph 1 (London: British Library, 1979).

Snodin, Michael, and John Styles, *Design and the Decorative Arts: Tudor and Stuart Britain, 1500–1714* (London: V&A Publications, 2004).

Stearn, William T., and Frederick A. Roach, *Hooker's Finest Fruits: A Selection of Paintings of Fruits by William Hooker (1779–1832)* (London: Prentice Hall, 1989).

Stokes, Jo, and Donald Rodger, *Heritage Trees of Britain and Northern Island* (London: Constable, 2004).

Tanaka, Seno, and Sendo Tanaka, *The Tea Ceremony* (Tokyo: Kodansha International, 1998).

Tichelaar, Pieter Jan, *Fries Aardewerk Tichelaar Makkum*, 2 vols (Leiden: Primavera Press, 2004).

Titchmarsh & Goodwin, *Fine English Furniture including the Georgian and Regency Period* (Ipswich: Titchmarsh & Goodwin, 2012).

Turner, Michael, *Eltham Palace Guidebook*, (London: English Heritage, 1999).

Vijayan, K., 'Genetic Relationships of Japanese and Indian Mulberry (*Morus* spp.) Genotypes Revealed by DNA Fingerprinting', *Plant Systematics and Evolution*, 243 (2004), pp. 221–232.

Webster, Jeremy, and Grayson Perry, *The Charms of Lincolnshire*, exhibition catalogue, produced in collaboration with The Collection, Lincoln (Lincoln: Lincolnshire County Council and the Arts Council of Great Britain, 2006).

Wells, Diana, *Lives of the Trees: An Uncommon History* (New York: Algonquin Books, 2010).

White, Roger, 'Tissington Hall, Derbyshire', *House & Garden*, August 2012, p. 69.

Williams, Diane M. (series editor), *Plas Mawr, Conwy Guidebook* (Cardiff: Cadw, Welsh Assembly Government, 2008).

Winch, Dinah, *The British Galleries, 1500–1900: A Guide Book* (London: V&A Publications, 2001).

Survey List of Mulberry Trees in England and Wales

1 Kelmscott Manor, Lechlade, Gloucestershire (*Morus nigra*)
2 Scotney Castle, Lamberhurst, Tunbridge Wells, Kent (*Morus nigra*)
3 Hogarth's House, Chiswick, London (*Morus nigra*)
4 Sudeley Castle, Winchcombe, Cheltenham, Gloucestershire (*Morus nigra*)
5 Quenby Hall, Hungarton, Leicester, Leicestershire (*Morus nigra*)
6 Erddig Hall, Wrexham, Clwyd (*Morus nigra*)
7 Christ's College, Cambridge, Cambridgeshire (*Morus nigra*)
8 Chastleton House, Moreton-in-Marsh, Oxfordshire (*Morus nigra*)
9 Priest's House Museum, Wimborne Minster, Dorset (*Morus nigra*)
10 Fenton House, London (*Morus nigra*)
11 Athelhampton House, Dorchester, Dorset (*Morus nigra*)
12 Iford Manor, Bradford-on-Avon, Wiltshire (*Morus nigra*)
13 Charlecote Park, Wellesbourne, Warwick, Warwickshire (*Morus nigra*)
14 Down House, Downe, Kent (*Morus nigra*)
15 Painswick Garden, Gloucestershire (*Morus nigra*)
16 Westwood Manor, Bradford-on-Avon, Wiltshire (*Morus nigra*)
17 Dunham Massey, Cheshire (*Morus nigra*)
18 Painshill Park, Cobham, Surrey (*Morus nigra*)
19 The George, Stamford, Lincolnshire (*Morus nigra*)
20 Loseley Park, Guildford, Surrey (*Morus nigra*)
21 St Fagans National History Museum, Cardiff, South Glamorgan (*Morus nigra*)
22 Breamore House, Fordingbridge, Hampshire (*Morus nigra*)
23 Ascott House, Leighton Buzzard, Bedfordshire (*Morus nigra*)
24 Mapperton Gardens, Beaminster, Dorset (*Morus nigra*)
25 Melford Hall, Long Melford, Sudbury, Suffolk (*Morus nigra*)
26 Berkeley Castle, Berkeley, Gloucestershire (*Morus nigra*)
27 Middleton Hall, Tamworth, Staffordshire (*Morus nigra*)
28 Hellens, Much Marcle, Ledbury, Herefordshire (*Morus nigra*)
29 Rochester Cathedral, Rochester, Kent (*Morus nigra*)
30 Upton House and Gardens, near Banbury, Oxfordshire (*Morus nigra*)
31 The Old Rectory, Warham, Wells-next-the-Sea, Norfolk (*Morus nigra*)
32 Hatfield House, Hatfield, Hertfordshire (*Morus nigra*)
33 Anglesey Abbey, Lode, Cambridge, Cambridgeshire (*Morus nigra*)
34 Great Dixter, Northiam, Rye, East Sussex (*Morus nigra*)
35 Broadlands, Romsey, Hampshire (*Morus nigra*)

36 Belchamp Hall, Sudbury, Essex (*Morus nigra*)

37 Squerryes Court, Westerham, Kent (*Morus nigra*)

38 Hever Castle, Edenbridge, Kent (*Morus nigra*)

39 Antony House, Torpoint, Cornwall (*Morus nigra*)

40 East Bergholt Place, East Bergholt, Suffolk (*Morus nigra*)

41 Dudmaston Hall, Quatt, Bridgnorth, Shropshire (*Morus nigra*)

42 Rockingham Castle, Market Harborough, Leicestershire (*Morus nigra*)

43 Hardwick Hall, Chesterfield, Derbyshire (*Morus nigra*)

44 Canons Ashby, Daventry, Northamptonshire (*Morus nigra*)

45 Bishop's Palace, Wells, Somerset (*Morus nigra*)

46 Fulham Palace, London (*Morus nigra*)

47 Langstone Court, Llangarron, Ross-on-Wye, Herefordshire (*Morus nigra*)

48 The Shakespeare Birthplace Trust, Stratford-upon-Avon, Warwickshire (*Morus nigra*)

49 Carshalton, Surrey (*Morus nigra*)

50 Archdeacon's Lodging, Christ Church, Oxford (*Morus nigra*)

51 Oxford University Botanic Garden, Oxford (*Morus alba*)

52 Canterbury Cathedral, Canterbury, Kent (*Morus nigra*)

53 Blickling Hall, Aylsham, Norfolk (*Morus nigra*)

54 Hayton, Carlisle, Cumbria (*Morus nigra*)

55 Basildon Park, Reading, West Berkshire (*Morus nigra*)

56 Winchester College, Winchester, Hampshire (*Morus nigra*)

57 Swallowfield Park, Reading, Berkshire (*Morus nigra*)

58 Grantham House, Castlegate, Grantham, Lincolnshire (*Morus nigra*)

59 Burghley House, Stamford, Lincolnshire (*Morus nigra*)

60 Tissington, Ashbourne, Derbyshire (*Morus nigra*)

61 Clevedon Court, Clevedon, Avon (*Morus nigra*)

62 Chipping Campden, Gloucestershire (*Morus nigra*)

63 Cliveden Gardens, Taplow, Berkshire (*Morus nigra*)

64 Exeter Community Centre, Exeter, Devon (*Morus nigra*)

65 Chichester Cathedral, Chichester, West Sussex (*Morus nigra*)

66 Tower House, Wells, Somerset (*Morus nigra*)

67 Eltham Palace, Greenwich, London (*Morus nigra*)

68 Broughton Castle, Banbury, Oxfordshire (*Morus nigra*)

69 Milton House, Stowmarket, Suffolk (*Morus nigra*)

70 Holehird Gardens, Windermere, Cumbria (*Morus nigra*)

71 Croxteth Hall, Liverpool, Merseyside (*Morus nigra*)

72 Pembroke College, Cambridge, Cambridgeshire (*Morus nigra*)

73 Carlton Hall, Carlton-on-Trent, Newark, Nottinghamshire (*Morus nigra*)

74 Buckland Abbey, Yelverton, Tavistock, Devon (*Morus nigra*)

75 Torre Abbey, Torquay, South Devon (*Morus nigra*)

76 Peterborough Cathedral, Cambridgeshire (*Morus nigra*)

77 Renishaw Hall, Sheffield, South Yorkshire (*Morus nigra*)

78 Longner Hall, Uffington, Shrewsbury, Shropshire (*Morus nigra*)

79 Roof Gardens, Kensington, London (*Morus nigra*)

80 Keats House, Hampstead, Greater London (*Morus nigra*)

81 Gunby Hall, Spilsby, Lincolnshire (*Morus nigra*)

82 Dartington Hall Gardens, Totnes, Devon (*Morus nigra*)

83 Rodmarton Manor, Cirencester, Gloucestershire (*Morus nigra*)

84 Mulberry House, Pakenham, Suffolk (*Morus nigra*)

85 Waddesdon Manor, Aylesbury, Buckinghamshire (*Morus nigra*)

86 Tiptree Farm, Colchester, Essex (*Morus nigra*)

87 Exeter Cathedral, Devon (*Morus nigra*)

88 Milton's Cottage, Chalfont St Giles, Buckinghamshire (*Morus nigra*)

89 Levens Hall, Kendal, Cumbria (*Morus nigra*)

90 Walsingham Abbey, Little Walsingham, Norfolk (*Morus nigra*)

91 Winchester Cathedral, Hampshire (*Morus nigra*)

92 Tyntesfield, Wraxall, Bristol, Avon (*Morus nigra*)

93 Wightwick Manor, Wolverhampton, West Midlands (*Morus alba*)

94 Deanery Garden, Winchester Cathedral, Hampshire (*Morus nigra*)

95 Barrington Court, Ilminster, Somerset (*Morus nigra*)

96 Felbrigg Hall, Norwich, Norfolk (*Morus nigra*)

97 Temple Newsam House, Leeds, West Yorkshire (*Morus nigra*)

98 Standen, East Grinstead, Sussex (*Morus nigra*)

99 Fountains Court, London (*Morus nigra*)

100 Merton College, Oxford, Oxfordshire (*Morus nigra*)